Dedicated to
Craig Piprell
1954 - 1994

The writing of this book was the legacy left to me by my
close friend and colleague, Craig Piprell.
He planted the seeds, I watered and weeded.
My sincere thanks to Akiko and the
Piprell family - Cliff, Charie,
Colin, Clarke and Rhian.

The Story of Butchart Gardens

Cover and book design by Cindy E. Harnett and Lorianne M. Koch
Printed and bound in British Columbia, Canada

Cover photo: Butchart Gardens
Author photo: Darren Stone

Canadian Cataloguing in Publication Data

Preston, Dave, 1956 -
The Story of Butchart Gardens

ISBN 0-9699540-0-1

1. Gardens - British Columbia - history. 2. Canadian history - British Columbia - Victoria 3. Tourism - history - Victoria.

Visit HIGHLINE PUBLISHING at NetBC
http://www.netbc.com

To Judy,

THE STORY OF

Butchart Gardens

DAVE PRESTON

HIGHLINE PUBLISHING

ACKNOWLEDGEMENTS

I am extremely grateful for the help I received in writing this book. My heartfelt thanks and deepest love go out to Lesley, for support way above and far beyond her usual role of wife and best friend. I thank my daughters, Jenn and Debbie, for understanding that dad doesn't work from nine to five every day and that he sometimes spends more time in the office than in the backyard.

I'd like to thank Sid Tafler for his thoughtful editing; Suzanne Steele for gentle prodding and proofing; Cindy Harnett and Lorianne Koch for designing the book and helping me through the long eleventh hour; the staff of archives all over the country, especially James and Brian at the BCARS; the B.C. Legislature Library; the Maltwood Art Museum and Gallery; George Eastman House; Greg Evans; Mike and Maureen Hardgrave; Island Publishers, Lana Denoni & Visitor Publications, The Great Canadian Beer Festival Society; Robert Copeland & Spode; Tom Henry; Fred Speckeen; Darren Stone; Derrick Mallard; staff at the Ministry of Environment, Lands & Parks; and Fleming Printing Ltd. . . .

Thanks, also, to my parents, for realizing that this is the closest their son will ever come to having a proper job.

And, of course, respectful thanks to Jennie and Robert Butchart and their family, without whom there wouldn't have been a book to write.

1. The Early Days In Owen Sound 11

2. Time To Plant A Garden 27

3. The 1920s - A Time For Growth 64

Colour Photographs I 89

4. Roses And A Home 97

5. Royalty, And The End Of An Era 119

6. The Ross Era Begins .131

Colour Photographs II .137

7. Benvenuto In The Nineties 160

Photo Credits 195

Bibliography 196

Index 198

THE STORY OF BUTCHART GARDENS
– FACT OR FICTION?

WELCOME TO the world of Butchart Gardens. In researching this incredible story I've uncovered many "facts" and figures, countless anecdotes, and many "quotations" made by the Butchart family and their successors. Where possible, I've verified my information, checked the facts, and heard the tales first hand from employees and associates. However, when dealing with almost a century of history, and thousands of people, it is impossible to completely separate fact from fiction. Good legends, I suspect, have a good dose of both.

The gardens themselves, depending on whom you ask, seem to vary in size from twenty-five to seventy-five acres. The distance from the Gardens to Victoria is another elastic measurement, reportedly being anything from ten to twenty miles. Some of these "facts" I've tried to establish, while others will be the topic of debate and discussion for years to come.

I soon realized that my task was not to prove nor disprove. In a few cases this is impossible, as many answers have long been buried with the only people who could confirm or deny a "fact." The stuff of legend is what makes a good story, and the stuff grows here as quickly as a well-tended flower bed. Legends cannot be proved or disproved, merely recounted and enjoyed. Mystery and speculation only serve to make them more durable. Butchart Gardens is certainly a legend.

The recounting of legends has long been an oral tradition, especially here on Vancouver Island. I sincerely hope that by capturing some of this legend on paper I have not removed any of its legendary qualities. This is not the official story. Neither has it been aided, sponsored or endorsed by Butchart Gardens. It's simply a wonderful story, simply told.

L ATE ONE mid-December afternoon in 1950, an elderly woman looked out of the window of her home in Victoria, and softly whispered to her nurse: "I've never seen a more beautiful sunset." A moment later, she died.

The woman was Jennie Butchart, and during her eighty-two years on this earth she helped make a small corner of it so beautiful that almost a million people a year travel to see it. The legacy she left rivals the splendor of any sunset and Butchart Gardens continues to amaze visitors from around the world . . . it's a remarkable legacy, left by a remarkable woman. And one which her family continues to cherish.

Jeannette Foster Kennedy was born on February 26, 1868, in the downtown of fast-growing Toronto, Ontario. Her Canadian-born mother, Martha Kennedy, was of Irish origin but little is known of her Irish father, James Kennedy, except that he was a reasonably successful seed and commission merchant. His untimely death occurred the same year Jeanette was born.

Jennie, as she preferred to be called, lived with her mother at 168 King Street West, then later in a brick-built house at 56 George St. in St. David's Ward, just a short walk from the busy shore of Lake Ontario.

According to her family and friends, the young Jennie was "round-faced, rosy-cheeked, wide-awake and full of laughter." Though polite and well-mannered, she was an active child and not afraid to show her natural athletic skills. "I rode almost as soon as I could walk," she told a reporter years later, and she could drive a coach and horses, or a "four in hand" at a very young age.

At twelve years old she could outskate most boys her age, and at sixteen, Jennie blossomed into a sophisticated young lady, but still shunned parading with a parasol in favour of riding bareback ponies around the countryside. She was, it was said, "the best equestrienne in the park," and had an interest in all kinds of sport.

When her mother died in 1880, Jennie moved to Owen Sound, another busy Great Lakes port of the time, to live with her aunt, Mrs. Robert Paterson. Although there were seven other children in the family already, Jennie settled down quickly into her new home, and enjoyed outdoor life. She would help out on the farm and a favourite companion was a large collie dog, which helped Jennie chase and round up cattle; an illicit pastime that earned them both a frequent scolding.

"My aunt was an excellent housekeeper," she later recalled, "and we were taught domestic science in the good, old fashioned, unforgettable school of experience." The skills she learned in that basic kitchen would stand her in good stead, when later the world, as it would seem, began to visit her home and appreciate her role as gracious hostess.

Jennie's uncle Robert had moved to Ontario from his native Scotland in 1847, and soon became an influential member of local society. He served as the mayor of Owen Sound, and well-connected company for his family was never far away. Despite her Irish name, Kennedy, which comes from the Gaelic, *Ceinneidigh*, meaning "ugly head", Jennie was an attractive young woman, always popular, and extensively courted.

Often on the lookout for adventure, she had several ascents in hot air balloons, and was one of the first to sit at the controls of a "flying machine." She even flew with Louis Blériot, the French aviation pioneer who made the first solo aircraft crossing of the English Channel. Jennie was fascinated by the daring of Blériot, who only managed the crossing because a chance rain shower had cooled the overheating engine. No one would suspect that this woman, thrilled as she was with the high life, would later scold her husband and cancel the purchase order when he tried to buy a helicopter.

Jennie was artistically gifted and extremely bright, so it's hardly surprising to learn she attended one of the most prestigious schools in Canada. At least, the Canada of the 1880s. The Brantford Young Ladies' College was built in connection with the Presbyterian Church, by spending fifty thousand dollars to convert the luxurious, rambling home and grounds of the Honorable E. B. Wood, who'd recently left the place to become Chief Justice of Manitoba. With room for about eighty boarders, plus a few local day students, the college gained a reputation for its literature and fine arts programs, with awards being presented by British royalty on at least one occasion. Affluent students were attracted from across the continent, and among Jennie's ten classmates were young ladies from New Jersey, British Columbia and Quebec. She graduated in 1885 and, although her academic performance and talent as a painter won her a scholarship to study art in Paris, she never took the opportunity. At eighteen she already had another, more important, project in mind: marriage.

Robert Pim Butchart was a tall, lean young man of Scottish descent, with a good head for figures and a fine business career unfolding before him. Owen Sound, in the township of Sydenham, was a burgeoning port, first settled in 1840, as steamers were busily opening up this part of the continent via the Great Lakes.

Initially, the Scots had never really been excited about the "New World" but after 1770 many were leaving their home to seek asylum and a new life in Canada. During the 1850s they were arriving by the boatload to ply their trades and seek their fortunes. Between 1851 and 1855 approximately seven thousand people left Scotland for British North America, keen to find work as engineers and skilled labourers. Robert's grandfather, James Butchart, was among them. Born in the Forfar district of Scotland in 1805, he brought his wife Mary (née McLaughlin) and seven children to start a new life in Canada.

There were many Butcharts in the area, and most were doing well. Working together, the family prospered in the booming town, providing trades for settlers and shipping lines. James junior was a carpenter, David a tailor, and George McLauchlan Butchart, Bob's father, a tinsmith who established a thriving hardware store.

As a youngster, and eldest son of eleven children, Bob didn't take much of a shine to schoolwork, possibly because of a Mr. P. A. Black, a whiskery school master who apparently carried a rubber strap under his coat and "had no compunction about bringing it down on your arm smartly." After nine years he left the classroom, anxious to take his place behind the counter of the family business. His father, a town councillor and captain in the 31st Grey Battalion of Infantry, was

Capt. G.M. Butchart was a councillor, a businessman and strict father to Robert.

something of a disciplinarian. With his son's best interests at
heart, he insisted Bob return to studies, which he eventually
did, at the Owen Sound Collegiate.

The Owen Sound of that period wasn't a cheap place to
live. Roads were primitive and the railway hadn't arrived, so

15

groceries were about twice the price they were in major cities, such as Toronto. Natural resources were in abundance, however. Pigeons were especially plentiful, to the extent they occasionally "blocked out the sun" and were a staple in many a kitchen pot. Local deer, partridge and rabbit were also welcome pantry visitors, making hunting a useful, if not essential, pastime for the young men of the town. Bob was no exception, learning militia rifle skills at his father's side and taking fish with apparent ease from the lakes and rivers. Also, like his father who made "a good showing" in the first ever regatta in the area, Bob took to boating, with a love that would eventually land him a page or two in the history of Canadian shipbuilding.

Bob's father died in 1882, at the age of fifty-four, leaving his boys in charge of the busy hardware store, which had risen to dominate the business district of town.

Church attendance and associated social gatherings were requisite, and Bob soon became friendly with Jennie Foster Kennedy. Bob's father and Jennie's uncle Robert had been colleagues on the town council and active members of local society. Jennie and Bob's courtship was deemed to be a good match, and well encouraged.

In 1882, Bob started to look beyond the small realm of hardware sales, even though the Butchart business was doing well, having established two stores in the frontierland of Manitoba. Bob had bigger ideas, and after collecting all the investment capital he could lay his hands on, he set up a primitive cement works with J. M. Kilbourn at Shallow Lake, about nine miles northwest of Owen Sound.

Despite their best efforts and numerous consultations with "experts" in the new field of cement manufacture, this venture failed miserably. They couldn't get the recipe right and were guessing at the process for the most part. But so committed to the idea was Bob that he bought out his partners, and promised himself he'd find a solution to the manufacturing problem.

At twenty-seven years old, having outsmarted or out-maneuvered Jennie's other suitors, Bob Butchart won the hand of his eighteen year-old bride. They went down to Buffalo for the wedding and Jennie shelved any thoughts of furthering her career in visual arts, devoting herself instead to her new husband and providing support to this determined entrepreneur.

The wedding celebration was followed by a holiday in Europe, and during their stay in England Bob's industrial career took a short-cut. A new kind of cement was being made, quite successfully, in England, and Bob badly needed the recipe.

However, manufacturers of the new Portland Cement were understandably tight-lipped, and as an industrial spy Bob failed repeatedly, being turned away or shunned by such as the famous firm of White and Sons in Kent. But one day, while walking down a street in a small town, he noticed a store which advertised the new cement, and more importantly it advertised the name of its owner: a Mr. A. J. Butchart.

After some minutes of jovial conversation, it was established that A. J. and Bob were distant relatives, and shared the bond of the clan. It wasn't long before the secret recipe for making Portland Cement was discreetly revealed to him.

On his return to Canada, Bob scraped more financing together, formed a second partnership, and put the new manufacturing process into play. By 1888 he was turning out the first Portland Cement ever made in Canada, and on his way to becoming father of the Canadian Cement Industry.

Bob and his partners initially had a hard time convincing engineers of their product's quality. The biggest hurdle, it seemed, was the packaging, which they had changed from traditional wooden barrels to burlap sacks, (sacks were cheaper, easier to handle, more efficiently stowed, and weighed only a quarter of what the barrels weighed). But appearances aside, the new cement was ideal for a country still in the making. Bob kept close watch on his enterprise, and he and Jennie lived close to his first Ontario plant, on a small island off Owen Sound.

Despite a temperance movement that lacked nothing in gusto, Owen Sound, like many active ports, was gaining a reputation for its drinking problem. Eighty per cent of the adult population drank, earning Owen Sound the nickname "Corkscrew Town."

Genteel society and Church-based communities seemed to be in decline, so no doubt Jennie, who was now the mother of two young daughters, Jenny and Mary, would greet the chance to move away with her new husband when the right opportunity arose.

THE MOVE WEST

Almost three thousand miles away, at the other side of the country in British Columbia, a man called John Grieg had discovered lime deposits on the shores of Tod Inlet on southern Vancouver Island, and had run a small business providing local farmers and homesteaders. The operation was sold to a Robert Grey, who in turn passed it on to a local fishmonger called Joseph Wrigglesworth.

Wrigglesworth built a lime kiln there in 1890 and sent

North end of the limestone quarry, circa 1906. Ten years later it bloomed.

some rock samples back to his native England for analysis. The samples turned out to be of a grade ideal for making the new Portland cement and the market for this powdery white rock suddenly seemed a lot bigger, and more lucrative. Thanks to an agent named J. E. Murphy, word of this limestone deposit soon got back to Bob Butchart who came out to Victoria to see for himself the potential it held for his cement business.

Bob came out again to personally inspect the site in the late spring of 1903 and, after doing his homework and calculating the risk, he sent the following letter, as Manager of the Owen Sound Portland Cement Co. Ltd., to a Mr. W.E. Losee, his contact in Victoria.

                                        July 18, 1903
Dear Mr Losee:-

          On my arrival home about a week ago I found
your favor of the 30th ulto, and to-day am in receipt of your
letter of 8th inst. I should have written you earlier but
have been unable to get my men together and discuss the subject with them. We have decided to erect the plant at Tod
Inlet providing we can make suitable arrangements for future
supply of coal. I am pleased with your very full description of the Sooke River Power. It looks as if this power
can be developed at a reasonable cost. I have sent your figures to the Wm. Hamilton Co. who are to give me a figure for
suitable Samson Water Wheels. They say that with this fall
and head 1150 Horse Power can be developed with their Wheels.
Your suggestion to try and obtain the use of the water free
is a good one, and on my return to Victoria will take this
up with the Hon. Mr. McBride. We will require all the assis-
tance possible from the Government and Municipality because
I have just learned that the importations of cement into
British Columbia last year were only 40,455 bbls. The cost
per barrel to manufacture this small quantity will be very
high. I hope the Electric Railroad to the head of Saanich
Inlet may become an assured fact and that it may run close
past the cement works. It will be very convenient for our
Employees. We will have to run chances that they do not get
on to our Sooke River Power. If cutting the timber over the
transmission line will not cost more than $100 per mile we
will be getting of pretty safe.

          Sorry to hear that you have contracted such a bad cold
and trust you are quite better.

          Your sketch showing Ferry slip noted. I am not sure
if it will not pay us to purchase a barge to carry our coal
and also to use the barge for conveying the cement to
Victoria, Vancouver, and elsewhere. I am not sure what time
I will return to Victoria. Am awaiting a letter from
nanaimo. In the meantime am getting figures on machinery,
etc. Thank you very much for the valuable information you
have been able to get me. Trusting it may prove profitable
to both of us, I remain, with kind regards,

          Yours truly,
          (sig.) R.P.Butchart

20

With that, a decision was made to move the Butcharts and their young family out to British Columbia, to start a new life – and a garden.

Land at the time was fairly cheap, around seven dollars an acre, so Bob also bought the neighbouring Peter Fernie farmstead, a quiet, waterfront property with a small cottage and a couple of rustic outbuildings. He retained the farm's Chinese employees and kept the original lime kiln in use for a while, using it to build the coarse walls of the first cement factory. It was to be the start of a huge, lucrative industry for the Butchart family, but it was also a very sad time for homesick Jennie, who missed her eastern family and friends terribly.

When Bob first took Jennie out to the site, over the dusty, bumpy trail known then as Limekiln Road, she didn't know what to expect. "We drove out with a span of horses and had a picnic lunch at the inlet," she told Maclean's Magazine, years later. "Where the house and upper garden are now was a deep ravine with steepish banks. I sat there having our picnic and crying with loneliness. I wanted to go home to Ontario."

But the landscape of British Columbia charmed her, as it has done so many travellers and new arrivals, and the lush green slopes were an enchanting, enticing backdrop. "It was very pretty, that ravine, and the woods all around, and the view of the inlet. After a while I agreed to stay and try it."

WELCOME TO SAANICH

Saanich covers almost seventy square miles of a peninsula on southern Vancouver Island, and was the winter home of some Northern Straits Salish Indians. "Saanich," in their Sencoten dialect, meant "fertile." Huge Douglas fir trees cov-

The wharf at Tod Inlet - until roads improved, this dock often saw more Garden-bound visitors than cement plant workers.

ered the steep slopes of Mount Newton, whose thousand foot summit dominated the landscape. To the north and south, gently rolling areas were ideal for homesteading, with rich soil and a moderate climate. Beaches to the east were smooth and good for shellfish and crabs, while to the west the shore was steeper, falling away into the depths of Saanich Inlet with its teeming fishery.

Natural resources were plentiful, with game, such as deer, being a major food source for the Salish, who also ate dried salmon with dried berries, waterfowl, shellfish and sea-weed.

Sir James Douglas, the Hudson Bay Trading Company factor who built Fort Victoria in 1843, expected new immigrants would swallow up pastoral Saanich as they rolled the boundary of Victoria northward. But immigrants didn't always care for city life.

Many of Saanich's first settlers and pioneers were fiercely independent, and not given to falling into uniform communities. In fact, most came here to start a new life away from rules and restrictive municipal disciplines. Some were fleeing the oppressive class structure of Victorian England, to carve a livelihood out of a bountiful wilderness, where owning a patch of land was quite within their reach. Others were retiring from organizations such as the Hudson's Bay Company, or leaving the British Navy. The Royal Sappers were dispatched to build the early roads of Saanich, and many stayed on when their work was finished, keen to put down roots and call the place home.

There were a few prospectors, too, who came north from San Francisco, dabbled in a nearby gold find at Leechtown near Sooke, but saw that raising chickens and planting orchards was an easier life than digging for nuggets.

Early Saanich saw natives and white settlers work and trade with each other in a spirit of cooperation. The Butcharts moved to an area where neighbour helped neighbour and the challenge of establishing a whole new community, let alone an industry, was met with many helping hands.

The Laboratory at the cement works — Jennie Butchart and her daughter worked here as assistant chemists.

THE TOD INLET CEMENT WORKS

Work began on construction of the cement plant in March 1904, and a few weeks later, on April 19, The Vancouver Portland Cement Company Limited was formed with a $500,000 capital investment. A Toronto financier, Mr. E. R. Wood was president, with Bob taking on the role of managing director plus many other duties. Another newcomer from Ontario, twenty-six year-old Mr. Harry A. Ross, was appointed treasurer, and would soon earn a place in the Butchart family.

Many other skilled workers were brought in and employment opportunities were welcomed by the region. The deep, safe waters of Saanich Inlet were ideal for getting supplies in and out of the plant, and by March 1905, the first sacks of Portland cement weighing almost ninety pounds each, were making their way by the barge *Alexander*, to a waiting market.

Business took off almost immediately. The strength of cement as a building material had been tested in the east and now local engineers and builders were anxious to get their hands on some. By spring of 1906, Bob's cement business was booming. A daily newspaper report of the time said:

"R.P. Butchart, manager of the Vancouver Island Portland Cement Company at Tod Creek, this morning said that he was working night and day to supply the local demand, and has ordered another mint which is now on its way here. He will increase the plant from six hundred barrels, and will supply the Canadian trade before filling orders for San Francisco, although builders there are offering seventy-five cents to one dollar more a barrel just now."

The San Francisco fire had builders there crying out for cement, and willing to pay a premium for it. Bob refused to take advantage of the situation, insisting that local builders and engineers were to be supplied first, even if Californians were offering up to a dollar more per barrel. The steamer *Trader* did set sail from Tod Inlet with one load for the States but much more was already on its way from Europe.

New equipment was ordered and the plant was enlarged again, with production increasing by another fifty per cent to nine hundred barrels a day. Alberta was also hungry for cement, and by September 1906 Bob was heading out to

Calgary to help establish another manufacturing plant there. "We expect to be in running shape by June 1st next," he told a reporter, "and there is a very good outlook for the product. The country in that part of Canada is building up rapidly, and the works will doubtless be operated to capacity."

Hydro electricity, too, was an ally in Bob's venture. Architects soon realized that electric elevators could replace stairs and carry people quickly and easily—buildings became taller, and the demand for cement increased again. Municipal authorities were also finding that wooden boardwalks were expensive to maintain, so they ripped them up and replaced them with smooth, level cement sidewalks. To add to all this, motor vehicles had arrived, bringing with them increased wear and tear on roads and bridges, which would soon be made more durable, thanks to cement. By 1916 there would be sixty times as much roadway paved as there had been in 1909.

The last frontier of the Dominion of Canada was now enjoying phenomenal growth and finally had its own supply of the precious building material, which would place it alongside the other "civilized" regions of twentieth century North America.

But like many industrialists of that boom time, Bob was having trouble finding a steady supply of labour for his plant. He was often under-staffed, and had to achieve more with less. Despite hiring hundreds of Chinese and fifty or so East Indians for labouring jobs, this staffing problem delayed installation of the new kiln. However, the early years were lucrative and a bustling little village sprang up on the banks of Tod Inlet.

Although she was proud of her husband's success, Jennie mentioned, only half jokingly, the price the environment was paying. "You're ruining the country, Bob," she said, "just to get your old cement!"

WHILE THE cement works churned out valuable grey powder and smoked its way to financial success, Jennie was looking at an area being devastated by industry. The old Fernie farmhouse and outbuildings were down across a meadow in the northwest corner of the property, more accessible by boat than road, so work on a new house for the Butcharts had begun almost immediately in 1904. She and Bob had a small home with surrounding verandah built near the quarry, but they spent only the summer months there, living the rest of the year in Victoria or travelling.

"Our first little house was a cottage of only three rooms," said Jennie. As for gardening she was the first to admit she "knew nothing at all." But her friend, James Lawson, gave her a few sweet pea seeds and she bought some Caroline Testout roses from the Layritz Nurseries, to brighten the yard next to her new home. "So wild it was that the deer used to come right up to the door." These deer ate much of the garden, and would continue to do so for decades to come, (despite hundreds of locally-known tricks and ideas, and the

*The Butchart
estate sits at 48°34 North
and 123°28 West, pro-
tected from prevailing
westerly winds by
Malahat Mountain, and
by Willis Point and the
Partridge Hills which rise
to around eight hundred
feet on the far shore of
Tod Inlet.*

*The Gardens
enjoy a long, frost-free
growing season of almost
nine months in this sub-
Mediterranean climate.
Shrubs and trees here
tend to grow more quick-
ly and up to forty per
cent larger than they
would in parts of Europe
and the east coast of
North America.*

best efforts of nine head gardeners).

But Jennie wasn't deterred. "I had a small garden," she would later recall, "and I think it was that first horticultural venture, and seeing the marvellous way things grew out here where there were no cold winters, which started my enthusiasm."

Jennie soon learned, as do many migrants to Vancouver Island, that getting things to grow is often easier than getting them to stop growing.

The small garden flourished and soon expanded. Because of the natural slope of the land, broad terraces were made, with the surrounding rough ground being leveled out, stumps and brush removed and plantings made.

Part of the cement manufacturing process required clay, hauled from across what is now Wallace Drive, just east of Tod Inlet. As the clay was stripped for use in the factory, the larger

The Japanese·Garden – the first to be landscaped in 1906.

soil and sand particles were put aside, and Jennie had these piles gleaned to fill in the holes and craters of what would become the Upper Garden. A rough meadow soon became an expansive lawn. Tennis was highly fashionable at the turn of the century and an area of grass immediately behind the house was set aside for this genteel sport. The other lawn areas were used for croquet and, occasionally, archery.

The Butcharts called their home Benvenuto, Italian for welcome, and everyone who visited them certainly was. As the gardens grew, houseguests would ask if their friends could also visit, so just before the First World War, Bob and Jenny opened their gardens to the public, initially for just three days of the week. Word of mouth spread the news and tea was offered to all who came, with eighteen thousand people served in 1915. Jennie would often run around the outdoor tables herself with a teapot, making sure everyone was comfortable. If the weather was unusually harsh, visitors might be invited indoors, and Jennie came up with the idea of buying several umbrellas which would be loaned to any visitor caught in the rain, (this idea is still in use at Butchart Gardens today). It wasn't long before "visiting hours" were extended to five days a week, with the Butcharts keeping just Thursday and Sunday to themselves.

THE JAPANESE GARDEN

North of the Butchart home the sloping ground drops from around one hundred feet above sea level to a small, sheltered cove below. This little neck of Tod Inlet was ideal for mooring small boats and, given the state of local roads, it was often the preferred route of visitors to the household. They would tie up their boats and walk the few hundred yards up to the house. It seemed obvious, to Jennie at least, that this should be one of the next areas to receive careful attention, and work began in 1905.

Initially, the area was mostly stumps and brush, never having been properly incorporated into the adjacent farmland. Native salal and Oregon grape covered the sloping ground between tall Douglas fir, arbutus and Western cedar. It presented no small challenge, especially for what Jennie had in mind.

The Japanese style of garden was by now quite fashionable. Nearby Hatley Castle, built by wealthy coal baron James Dunsmuir, had employed a Boston company to develop its gardens, who in turn had employed the services of Isaboro Kishida to design a Japanese Garden there which still exists today. This talented Japanese landscape artist from Yokohama also designed a garden with tea rooms for the

Butchart's Japanese Garden incorporates many of the classic features which have inspired people for centuries.

The first Japanese Gardens were influenced by the Chinese, who formed a relationship with the natural world, expressed in their art, philosophy and religion. Stone is the most important element in the Japanese landscape but the other natural elements, sun, moon, stars, land, water and plants, each have their place in the overall scheme. Traditional plants include azalea, ferns, grasses, wildflowers and mosses, with trees coming from the cedar, cherry, fir, maple and pine families.

The Zen Buddhist garden had little colour or flowering material. This helped place the focus on their important tea ceremony. The teahouse, a peaceful haven in which to contemplate, is a legacy of this style.

The smiling clay Buddha found in the garden is by

Kenneth Bloomfield, a local artist, and is younger than it appears.

Early Japanese gardens were explored on foot or by boat, while the Zen gardens were designed to be enjoyed by a sitting visitor. Trees are trained to lean out and bend over, or weep, to frame a bridge or reflective pool of water.

All this has been achieved here, (with the help of two extensive renovations in 1961 and 1990) and even on the busiest days of summer it's possible to find a little peace and solitude in the cool, shady corners of the Japanese Garden.

The Butchart's daughter, Mary, in her early 30s,
shortly after her marriage to Charles Todd.

Gorge, Victoria's weekend society playground of the time.
Jennie, who was interested in the Orient and had travelled
there many times on her winter cruises, hired Isaboru Kishida
in 1906 to draft a design.

With the help of books and the guidance of more
knowledgeable friends, she planted Japanese maple trees, some
of which grow so slowly they have not been replaced to this
day. She marked the entrance with a grand, red lacquer gate,
or Torii, and planted copper beech trees at either side of it.

These trees are now among the oldest on the estate.

After she married, Jennie's daughter Mary hired a Scottish gardener, Hugh Lindsay, to create a garden around her new home on St. Charles Street in Victoria. Jennie was so impressed by his talent that she poached him away to become Benvenuto's first head gardener. Lindsay implemented the plans for the Japanese Garden, bringing it to the first stage of completion by 1910.

Jennie was confident enough to ignore the advice of Joseph Conder, who wrote in his 1912 book, *Landscape Gardening in Japan*: "Very rare flowers however beautiful, are not considered desirable material for gardens, the strange and unfamiliar being favoured only by vulgar and ignorant persons." Jennie, of course, was neither, and her Japanese Garden became a showpiece, and one of the rarest flowers of her time, the Tibetan Blue Poppy, grows there exquisitely.

On a June afternoon in 1917, the Natural History Society of Victoria drove out to Benvenuto in one of the large sight-seeing cars of the time, to be met and personally guided around the garden by Jennie. They reported: *"The Japanese garden with its multitude of dwarfed but sturdy shrubs was much admired, as were the little lakes and pools where trout of various kinds could be seen swimming in the clear water."*

THE NEW VILLAGE

Tod Inlet now had its own little community. The hastily-built shanty town of cabins with canvas roofs had soon become a village, housing over four hundred workers from the

The cement works loom over the south end of the new Sunken Garden.
Jennie planted the row of poplar trees to the right, to screen the buildings.

cement plant. The principal workers lived in small cottages just east of the wharf, (the foreman had a tennis court behind his, the remains of which can still be seen). The Chinese lived further east still, by Tod Creek, most of them in a huge bunkhouse that was later used by the Red Cross during the First World War. A small settlement of East Indians was just above, in a ramshackle collection of huts. There was a barn, stables and a field for growing hay, and many workers grew their own vegetables, and kept chickens or small livestock. They also planted fruit trees, some of which survive today.

Apart from a little fishing and hunting, the people of this new village were in need of entertainment. A two storey bunkhouse had been built for single men, with a large cook-house and dining room next door. This dining room was occasionally used for dances and card parties but was hardly ideal for community socializing. So in 1910, a few of the workers and locals formed the West Saanich Hall Committee and set about raising money to build a community hall. An obvious fundraiser was a garden party, which put almost forty dollars in the coffer, then Bob took an interest and donated two hun-

The eldest Butchart daughter, Jenny (lower right),
as bridesmaid for her friends Nellie Todd and
Alex Gillespie in 1907.

dred dollars. Plans for the concrete and wood hall were drawn
up and submitted to Bob, who not only gave some advice but
another fifty dollars to complete the project. The hall was a
huge success, used for dances, shows and other social functions. Bob's employees were active on the committee until the
Second World War, but in 1947 the society was folded and its
residue funds donated to a local church. The hall stood

approximately where the first Butchart Gardens sign and small garden are today, on the northwest corner of the Benvenuto Avenue and West Saanich Road intersection.

Before the Butcharts built a village here, the nearest post office was up on the main road, informally named after a pioneer family called Sluggett. Until the telephone became commonplace, a post office was the hub of nearly all communication, and a vital landmark. When Tod Inlet finally got its own post office this placed the village officially on the map of 1911. (Although it wasn't acknowledged by the Geographic Branch of the province until November, 1922, by which time the cement works had closed, most workers had left and the village was all but abandoned).

In summer, workers and their families were often treated to boat rides and short cruises around Saanich Inlet. At Christmas the children were remembered by Bob and Jennie with gifts of money and colourful sweaters. After they returned from a foreign trip there would often be tropical fruits or candy preserves to share among the youngsters.

The good will was reciprocated. Staff presented Bob with colouful flags and a pair of binoculars one Christmas, to use on his new motor launch. Then in 1923, the Butcharts were presented with a silver tea service inscribed "Land of Enchantment."

The Butcharts nurtured staff loyalty and many people spent a lifetime in employment at Benvenuto, often being followed into service by a son or daughter. It's a legacy that has continued, where staff meetings take the form of family gatherings, and after almost a century's operation there have been less than a dozen head gardeners.

BOB TAKES TO THE ROAD

Up to 1904 there was virtually no regulation of automobiles, but in February that year the "Motor Vehicles Speed Regulation Act" was passed, forcing registration of all vehicles. Each car was affixed with a permit number on the back, although there were only twenty-four in the whole province. On May 14 that year, Bob Butchart put down two dollars and bought himself a licence plate, number 11. According to blue ink handwriting in the leather-bound Register of Permits Motor Vehicles for that time, it was issued to "R J Butchart of Victoria."

The speed limit was ten miles per hour in any city, town or village, and fifteen miles per hour on any public highway outside, though a municipal bylaw could set aside any street or road for "testing" a vehicle at higher speeds.

The bleak winter of 1906 was brightened, for Bob at least, by the delivery of a new automobile. On February 23 he put down another two dollars to register a new licence plate, number 61, then took possession of a Thomas Flyer, a four-cylinder machine delivered by rail from the E. P. Thomas Company of Buffalo. Not only was this four-horsepower contraption the fastest car around, it was also one of the most expensive at $4,500, handsomely fitted with Russian leather and all the latest gadgets. It was advertised at forty miles an hour, though factory tests, and Bob, proved it could go faster, even over the narrow dirt roads of Saanich.

As he approached the age of fifty, Bob Butchart was about to become a speed king, and for the most part he got away with it. When Saanich Municipality was formed in 1906 there was only one policeman for its five thousand people: a Constable Russell, who patrolled his sixty-seven square mile beat on horseback, collecting both road and poll taxes. He

The first spring in the Sunken Gardens with lawns freshly sown.

probably got to know Bob, and his cars, quite well.

Horace Plimley, a mechanic from the city, once had to take the Thomas Flyer back to his garage to work on it, but couldn't drive it there as the lane out of the quarry was too rough and steep. So Bob had the car put on one of the cement barges and towed around to Victoria.

Supplies for the house and cement plant often came from Wilfred S. Butler's general store in nearby Keating. They were delivered, down the rugged and often treacherous Lime Kiln Road to Tod Inlet, by horse and cart, capably handled by Butler's delivery man Fred Chubb. Bob was impressed with Fred's driving skills and hired him to be his chauffeur, Chubb being issued official Chauffeur's Licence number 450 on July 31, 1912. It was renewed every year until 1916 although at least one incident had Fred wondering if he should perhaps return to the slower pace of horse-drawn traffic.

Bob was due at an important lunch meeting at the

Visitors enjoy the Upper Lawn in the 1920s.

Empress Hotel at 1:30 p.m. At 1:05 someone called from downtown to confirm that he'd attend the appointment. Bob took the call at home and promised he'd be there, bang on time. Racing out to the car he asked Fred to sit in the back while "Bullet" Butchart, as motoring friends now called him, pulled the throttle back "to the last notch" and drove the vehicle thirteen miles down a rough West Saanich Road, arriving at the hotel less than twenty minutes later. It's a feat that's difficult to accomplish even today—over paved expressway. Later, when lever-type throttles were replaced by pedals, the nickname "Leadfoot Bob" started doing the rounds.

Of course, accidents do, and did, happen. Bob's V-12 Packard which he "flew" around in was practically demolished after two years, (he liked it so much he ordered another, even though they weren't making them) and the vehicle bearing his original licence plate number 11 was registered as "Broken up - Butchart 8 May '07."

Jennie also took her turn behind the wheel. She was the second woman in Victoria to own an electric car, and reportedly drove more slowly than her husband, and with fewer incidents. When Bob reached the age of eighty, it is said that Jennie petitioned the police to take away his licence.

W. H. WESTBY – THE MAN IN THE QUARRY

The twentieth century brought with it affluence to many settled pioneers and industrialists. People who were doing well wanted to display their success via luxurious homes set among well-kept grounds. Landscape architecture was still in its Canadian infancy, but already much in demand by wealthy estate owners.

The term "Landscape Architect" had first been used in 1860 to describe the work of Frederick Law Olmstead, the man who designed New York's Central Park and Mount Royal Park in Montreal. As the Canadian Society of Landscape Artists wasn't formed until 1934, Jennie Butchart didn't have too many experts in the field from which to choose. Though luck was heading her way.

Born in Yorkshire in 1875, William Henry Westby began a career in gardening at twelve years old, apprenticing under his father who was head gardener at Welbeck Abbey, the Duke of Portland's estate. From there he went on to Renishaw Hall, an estate of over four thousand acres, frequently visited by King Edward VII, for whom Westby made a fresh boutonniere each morning. Trained in topiary and espaliery, he also learned to grow guavas and bananas. "There being no refrigeration then," he'd later say, "the big estates grew all sorts of their own tropical fruits."

Seeking a change in climate, (to aid the health of his son, Bill) Westby emigrated to Canada, moving to Winnipeg in 1912. A couple of years later, perhaps after realizing the harsh prairie climate wasn't what the doctor ordered, he came across to Victoria, where he'd been asked to start a nursery. His reputation reached the Butcharts and he was soon working to help fulfill Jennie's dream of transforming the old quarry. The plans for a towering rock garden, with pockets of perennials were largely his, and he helped turn her vision into

Winter bares the bones of the "rock island" in the early Sunken Garden.

colourful reality.

His son Bill helped out at the Gardens for a couple of years, before going to the local shipyards during the war. When he returned he apprenticed under his father and in 1922 the two of them left the Butcharts' employ to establish their own firm at Elk Lake, W. H. Westby & Son Landscape Gardeners and Garden Architects.

They did much work in the affluent Uplands area of Victoria, and one of their first big commissions came two years later when they took on the job of landscaping Crystal Gardens. This innovative glass and steel structure, behind Victoria's Empress Hotel, was a major building project, incorporating the largest indoor swimming pool in North America, plus a restaurant, ballrooms and indoor gardens. It was also the city's largest conservatory. "Everywhere . . ." read a news report of the time, "it is the intention to concentrate upon flowers."

The Westby's experience at Butchart Gardens stood them in good stead and they filled Crystal Garden's two and a

half acres of space with a magnificent display of ferns, begonias, azaleas and bougainvillea. Palms and Japanese Maple
were carefully placed to soften the building's hard lines, and
the complex was warmly received when it opened in 1925,
making the $250,000 Crystal Gardens "a veritable garden par-
adise." At each corner of the huge swimming pool stood a
stately arbor vitae; the same tree that became the hallmark of
Jennie's Sunken Garden.

CREATING THE SUNKEN GARDEN

A couple of years before Europe would erupt in "the
war to end all wars," Jennie looked out over the first quarry at
the end of her garden and saw a sight that filled her with
despair. All the useful limestone had been removed by 1908,
and the ravaged quarry was now an ugly, gaping hole, cover-
ing three and a half acres.

Excavation work had moved east to another part of the
property, leaving this rough quarry floor strewn with broken
machinery, discarded tools and assorted, rusting debris. A
towering island of rock stood silently in the centre, being of
too poor a grade to be useful to the cement plant, and behind
it gaped a huge crater where the limestone seam had run much
deeper. A small stream trickled its way across this site, form-
ing deep pools and muddy puddles. Scattered across it all were
hundreds of jagged rocks that had escaped the crusher, or been
ignored by the quarrymen.

As devastating as the scene was, this "silent, ghastly
tomb" gave Jennie inspiration, and a vision: "Like a flame, the
limestone pit burst into imaginary bloom. A flame for which

The Sunken Garden on a late summer's afternoon in 1928 - sometimes a little too popular with lovers waiting to watch the moon rise.

I shall ever thank God." A friend threw down a challenge by saying: "Even you would be unable to get anything to grow in there."

In 1910, Jennie tried to screen the cement works from view by planting a few Persian plum trees, and a row of Lombardy poplar that have survived to this day. The cement boom was beginning to slow, and many of the four hundred or so workers were frequently short of work. Jennie asked Bob if a few of them could be seconded to her project, and soon many Chinese labourers, directed by William Westby, were hauling rocks and laying the foundations of flower beds and rock gardens.

A landscape consultant named Cole, from Washington came up with a design for the east section, by the waterfall, and Raoul Robillard later designed the more formal areas. Small retaining walls were built and thousands of tons of rich black topsoil, brought in by horse and cart from the neighbouring farmland, was piled behind them to form small beds.

The work was arduous and dirty. Mud plagued the wagon wheels and teams of horses strained to get their loads across the uneven quarry floor. Planks were laid down across the muddy patches and Westby struggled to lay drainage pipes along the rugged terrain, leading water away to a pond at the deepest end of the quarry, to the south. It was fenced off for safety and later became the site of the Ross Fountain.

A crater left in the middle of the quarry was lined and filled with water to form a tranquil lake, reaching depths of fifty feet in places. Bob, a keen fisherman, had an idea to stock the lake with trout, and the first few were caught in buckets from nearby Durrance Lake. Later, he took to aquaculture more seriously and ordered some young fish from the local hatcheries. He particularly liked rainbow trout and eventually trained these fish to come to the sound of his hands clapping, to be rewarded with food. It is said that Jennie's quest to lay a carpet of flowers and grass around the quarry lake was spurred on by the mud brought into her home on Bob's feet after a quarry fishing trip.

Bob had fished, quite successfully, since his younger days in Ontario. In 1908, during a seventeen-day cruise with friends aboard the power yacht, *Calcite*, he earned this account from shipmate John McCormick: *"For the benefit of those who do not know him, I will say that Mr. Butchart in everyday life is a very quiet, dignified gentleman, devoted to the successful management of a very large business, and is the last man one would choose as an enthusiastic fisherman. But I am here to say that when he got his first strike there was not a word of criticism to offer for the way in which he conducted himself. He played that salmon for fifteen minutes, giving it all the chance a true sportsman could be expected to give; at*

First, lusty spring,
all dight in leaves
of flowers,
That freshly budded, and
new blossoms did wear,
In which a thousand
birds had built
their bowers.

EDMUND SPENSER
Faerie Queene

45

The Sunken Garden Lake looking north circa 1920. Benvenuto, the home, is behind the trees (centre).

the same time he handled his gear like an expert, bringing the fish to gaff without a sign of the usual awkwardness of the once-a-year fisherman."

Although he now fished in his own backyard, Bob was quite protective of his stocks. He came home one day to find visitors fishing for his trout in the Sunken Garden. He was furious and chased them out, and reportedly closed that part of the estate to the public for several days.

Jennie's new horticultural venture took off, and the sharp tones of the quarry were soon being feathered by spirea, ferns, and "baby's breath." (Baby's breath was particularly apt, as its other name, *gypsophila*, means gypsum-loving—an ideal plant for a limestone quarry). Ivy and virginia creeper were planted into cracks in the walls, and the story goes that Jennie spent some time being dangled down the fifty-foot cliffs in a basketwork bos'n's chair, while she tucked tiny pieces of ivy into crevices.

Using a technique still employed by landscapers today, a watery mixture of soil and seed was splashed onto rocky surfaces and slopes, giving a tenuous grip for flowers of many colours. Plants such as thrift and stonecrop soon took hold of their lofty perches, and Jennie planted a pair of Asian bolleana white poplars which would shoot up to reach well above the quarry's rim, where they still tremble in the breeze today.

Help from the cement works' labour force was still forthcoming, as they were seconded to help plant a garden that would fast become a legend. Climbing roses were trained along bailing wire fastened over rocks and boulders, as they still are today. Around the lake and stream that fed it, masses of Japanese irises were planted, and lilypads soon covered the water's surface.

After about two years' hard work, the new garden was ready to be unveiled to the public, and people were amazed. Already the harsh lines of the quarry walls were disappearing beneath lush new growth. A fallen tree formed a rustic archway over the northern entrance and steps were cut into the steep bank at that end of the garden. Stepping stones down to the quarry floor were almost covered, and held in place, by saxifrages, starry-faced sedums, linums and portulacas.

Soft green lawns surrounded flower beds and rockeries teemed with colour. A tiny flagstone bridge took visitors over the stream that fed the lake, already ringed by healthy young trees. Boulders that once littered the quarry floor now formed small islands in a verdant sea, shading low-light plants and conserving moisture on one side, while providing a warm home to sun-loving plants on the other.

The first tea room (there were several around the estate eventually) was perched high on the southeast rim of the quarry, offering a wonderful view of the new garden and Tod Inlet. In 1921 the Sunken Garden was finished, and people could hardly believe the transformation.

For the first few years, visitors simply roamed around the lawns but as the flower beds grew in size, foot traffic was increasingly forced through narrowing areas, and the grass began to wear down. As visitors increased so did the problem and, much to Jennie's chagrin, flagstone pathways were eventually laid. Years later these were replaced by permanent cement and cobblestone footpaths, which in turn had to be widened to their present size.

The two trees which flank the pathway are arbor vitae (also known as Western red cedars) and although they're not the most unusual trees on the estate, they've become a feature which makes the Sunken Garden instantly recognizable the world over. They are not pruned but grow naturally in a tight, conical shape. Bob planted the first pair here in 1920, but over the years, as they increased in height, casting too much shadow and obscuring the view from the lookout, they have been replaced several times.

A FAMILY AFFAIR

During the first few years at Tod Inlet, Bob was very much in control of the cement works. His jobs included timekeeper, paymaster, general foreman and plant manager. He was very much a "hands-on" boss and even with his quiet

Letterhead from the Butcharts' cement company. It's huge success allowed over $100,000 to be spent developing the Gardens.

voice, he only had to say things once. Like many successful businessmen, Bob didn't suffer fools gladly, if at all, and he contained a fiery temper that would erupt if things didn't go according to plan. Once, down on the wharf behind the plant, he grabbed a workman by the overalls and threw him off the dock into the frigid waters of Tod Inlet. He immediately apologized and made sure the man was rescued.

All four of the Butchart family were involved in the daily running of things. Jennie and her daughter Jenny helped Mr. Highberg, the works chemist, in the simple, one-room laboratory, testing rock and cement samples for content and quality. Mary Butchart worked as record keeper, and in August 1910, at the age of twenty-two, she married William Charles Todd, son of Bob's close friend, Charles Fox Todd. At twenty-five, Charles was already a manager of his father's successful fish company, and had a house built for his new wife at the prestigious address of 944 St. Charles Street, Victoria. (Real estate had been booming, and during the six years up to 1912, quarter-acre lots in Victoria's Fairfield district had shot up from four hundred to five thousand dollars).

Butchart Cove, as peeked from the Japanese Garden.

Harry Ross, the company's treasurer since 1904, became a close family friend, as well as colleague. At the age of thirty-nine, on January 15, 1917, he took the hand of thirty-two year-old Jenny Butchart in marriage. The Right Reverend Charles Schofield, Bishop of Columbia, officiated at the ceremony, held at Christchurch Cathedral in Victoria. Bob, Jennie, Mary and Charles Todd were witnesses.

A noted Vancouver Island naturalist of the time, Robert Connell, toured the gardens during a bleak winter's day in January, 1931.

PEACE DOVES

THIS BRONZE STATUE
IS PLACED AT THE
SITE OF MR. BUTCHART'S
PIGEON HOUSE

His visit was cheered considerably after leaving the Sunken Garden with its frozen ponds and frosty lawns. *"Returning by another path, the voice of singing birds came through the wintry air and I caught a glimpse of a peacock's tail. In a roomy aviary were two or three peafowl with a flock of beautiful mallards and a company of pigeons as varied in form as in colour. Looking at the aviary from the upper end with the quaint pigeon houses...the green, blue and bronze of the peacocks in the foreground, the soft pearly greys and blues of the pigeons, I seemed to see an Old World picture, and breathe the calm and placid atmosphere of a bygone age. And still comes through the air the song of the birds."*

Robert Butchart's love of boats, and his grandson's time in the navy, are echoed in the Butchart Gardens' sign - as a porthole in a wooden boat hull.

Bob's close friend, Charles Todd, was a member of the Natural History Society of B.C. which in 1901 had proposed a paper titled *Introduction of Useful Birds*. Many residents were recently off the boat from England and Scotland and missed the fauna of their homeland, and hedgerows alive with bird-song.

More importantly, it seemed, many European birds were fond of insects, and would be useful pest-controllers to farmers who were settling the area. Of course, mention was also made as to their singing ability and the narrow, winding lanes of Saanich had reminded more than one writer of rural England.

The provincial government finally gave the society five hundred dollars, half the estimated cost of importing such birds as the skylark, goldfinch, robin, siskin, nightingale and blue tit. Bob Butchart, however, was to spend a lot more than that on importing his feathered friends.

Bob was a keen bird fancier, despite being somewhat allergic to them, (they gave him asthma). However, he continued the society's movement with gusto, bringing in exotic birds from all over the world. Soon the Gardens were ringing to the sound of birdsong, and noisy peacocks wandered the pathways and roosted in trees, oblivious to the traffic of the estate bustling around them.

In March, 1927, Jennie and Bob were visiting England when they were enthralled by the singing of some caged birds. Bob placed an order and two months later a shipment of English and Mexican canaries and a pair of piping bullfinches were riding the rails of the CPR across Canada. The birds were valued at thousands of dollars and received special treatment on their journey, with progress being reported almost daily by the local press.

However, thanks in part to a report in *The Daily Province*, the importation drew criticism and fears of undesirable birds being let loose to breed and cause irreparable damage to the Island's ornithology. Bob wasted no time in defending his feathered shipment.

In an open letter, published on August 27, 1927, he corrected one ill-informed critic. ". . . *So that you may not be unnecessarily alarmed, I might say there were no jackdaws in the consignment . . . neither were there any other harmful species of birds. Three hundred birds is an exaggeration, as only 101 were in the consignment, and these birds are not to be turned out into the garden, as your letter suggested, but are now housed in a comfortable aviary, where, I hope, they will*

One of the Butchart aviaries (right, behind the gazebo), ran along the Italian Gardens' east side — until it was replaced by a bowling alley.

be very well cared for and give much pleasure, as they are now doing to our garden visitors." The case was closed.

Bob had bird cages lining Benvenuto's indoor swimming pool room, expensively appointed with bronze and marble, and trained pigeons lived on the site of what is now the Begonia Bower. A special pond was to be built for his growing collection of ornamental ducks and Bob had a luxurious house designed especially for them by a leading architect.

On his return from one boating trip, as he walked up from the inlet, a large green parrot flew down from the roof of the house and perched on the shoulder of his daughter, coming across the lawn to greet him. A loud parrot was generally at large in the house. (Ann-Lee Ross, wife of Bob's grandson Ian, later admitted to being terrified of this bird, or one like it, that ruled the Butchart dining room many years ago).

THE STORY OF BUTCHART GARDENS

A NATURAL WINNER

Bob liked to play cards and would often challenge members of the household staff to a game of rummy. It didn't take the servants long to figure out that he liked to win, which he usually did. Quite often in the evenings, he'd play a hand or two of cribbage with Jennie, for a one dollar stake. Bob always won the game and would proudly claim the dollar bill, tucking it safely into his pocket before retiring to bed. However, after he'd undressed, Jennie would secretly retrieve the bill and hide it until they next played, when out it would come to be used as her bet. Apparently without knowing it, Bob won the same dollar bill back many times, and Jennie always "lost" it to him with good humour.

Bob's head for figures and card-playing ability also stood him in good stead with many business deals. News of the Portland Cement industry boom didn't take

When lovers strolled in the Italian Garden at dusk, Robert Butchart, hidden from their view in the house, would turn on concealed lights and play romantic organ music.

Bob was an aspiring musician himself. He owned a violin but his talent, according to Jennie, was sorely lacking. On one occasion she silenced his practice by putting soap on his bow, and later, in a fit of frustration, he smashed the instrument.

Jennie's peace was short-lived, however, as Bob then took up the mouth organ. She said it was even worse than the violin.

long to reach England, and soon a UK firm had plans to start Bamberton, a rival cement plant, right across the water from Tod Inlet.

The First World War had slowed demand for cement and Bob's plant was heading for fierce competition with the new company. Tod Inlet had the edge on marketing, and negotiations were begun on cooperation between the two cement works. Bob often grew explosively angry in meetings which led to a mediator being brought in from England.

The deal turned out well for Bob, who'd had an ace up his sleeve—what the Bamberton company didn't know was that the Tod Inlet plant would soon be exhausted. Because he could only excavate a specified distance from the railway line at the east side of his property, Bob was rapidly running out of limestone (he'd had diamond drillers in to determine exactly how much was left).

The two companies finally agreed to a cooperative merger, with Bob becoming head of the new concern. Rather than compete and flood the market with cement, Bamberton was put on hold while the Tod Inlet plant continued for a few more years.

Before the tour bus age, visitors cruise up Tod Inlet to the Gardens. The cement works' dock is straight ahead, on the left shore.

THE BUTCHART BOATS

My garden is a forest ledge
Which older forests bound
The banks slope down to the blue lake-edge
Then plunge to depths profound
RALPH WALDO EMERSON - My Garden

One of the easiest ways to get to Butchart Gardens until the 1920s was by boat. Most bulky supplies came and went from the cement works via water, which let Bob indulge in his passion for boats.

Much of the equipment used to build the cement works, and much of the cement it made, was carried by barges pulled by tugs. One of the first ships Bob bought, in 1905, was *Beatrice*, a fourteen-year-old schooner—a great deal at $625 (and 80 years later it still served as a marine biology research vessel). Scows brought coal in loads of 300 tons to the cement works, towed by the tugs *Sadie, Spray, Swell,* and *Edna Grace.*

In 1910 he bought the *Marmion*, an iron and steel

schooner-rigged steamer from Scotland which he used to carry gypsum from Alaska, and cement from the works. A year later the vessel made headlines by running aground in Vancouver, taking out two vital water mains in the process. However, the boat was to redeem itself.

During the last week of January, 1916, a rare winter storm left six feet of snow on the ground, bringing all traffic, including both railways, to a complete standstill for days. The village of Tod Inlet seemed cut off from the world. The *Marmion* came to the rescue, making a mercy run around Saanich Inlet to the town of Sidney to bring in supplies.

In 1912 the *S.S.Leona* joined Bob's fleet as his cement production reached its peak of about half a million barrels a year. She was used to bring bags of salt from San Francisco to Victoria, and gypsum to the cement works, until being lost during a storm in Active Pass, along with seven of her crew.

The *Bamberton* was a fifty-foot ship built in Victoria during 1913, especially for the Bamberton cement works. She was used as a commuter vehicle, ferrying employees across to their jobs on the west side of Saanich Inlet.

Since his days on the Great Lakes back east in Ontario, (and despite losing his eldest sister, Mary Jane, in the sinking of the *S.S. Aggoma* in 1885) Bob Butchart had always been a keen sailor and knew his way around a ship. In April, 1909, he treated himself to a four thousand dollar motor yacht, the Seattle-built *Iloilo*, which a local paper described as *"one of the trimmest and most handsomely appointed launches on the Sound, built four years ago at a cost of about $11,000 . . . 60 feet long and 12 feet beam, finished in oak and furnished in blue velvet, equipped with electric lights. She will carry about 125 passengers and has berths for thirteen persons."*

It was Bob's pride and joy, which he kept moored in the inlet and frequently used to entertain visiting naval officers.

His seamanship, and head for business, also landed him a powerful and prestigious position towards the end of the First World War.

Together with his friend Captain J. W. Troup, he was asked by the Imperial Munitions Board to direct shipbuilding for British Columbia. This position took him away from home on many occasions, and he fought hard with national government to have new ships made of local Douglas fir, as opposed to iron and steel. It was a stressful time for Bob, as he tried to award contracts fairly, between competing yards in Victoria and Vancouver.

Tod Inlet was always busy with vessels of all sizes, commercial and pleasure. In 1919, Bob had noted architect Samuel Maclure design, at considerable expense, a classic-style boathouse—an attractive structure that stood for years, only to sink, it is said, on the day that Bob's grandson, Ian Ross, had it insured.

In 1921, Bob's company bought the wooden, semi-diesel coastal freighter *Teco* and the beautiful, two hundred and forty foot motor schooner *Laurel Whalen*, which was launched with due ceremony in Victoria harbour. One of the last ships to be bought was the fateful *Island King*, launched in Norway in 1920 as *Granit*. It took her nine troublesome months to sail from Newcastle-on-Tyne to Vancouver Island, (and the captain was fined en route for carrying stow-aways). Meeting her at William Head on the Strait of Juan de Fuca, Bob took no chances on the last leg of her journey and had the vessel towed around to the Yarrows Shipyards in Victoria for an engine refit.

It is not by accident that the Butchart Gardens' sign resembles the porthole in a ship's hull.

TO THE GARDENS BY RAIL

When the Butcharts first came to Tod Inlet, the wood-fueled Victoria and Sidney Railway, nicknamed "The Cordwood Limited," had been running for a decade, but along the other side of the peninsula so it was of little use to them.

Then in 1910, the BC Electric Railway announced plans for new hydroelectric sources at Jordan River–it was this and the construction of a steam-powered auxiliary plant at Tod Inlet that finally gave them enough power to open a Peninsula line, connecting their successful streetcar system in Victoria with the booming population of Saanich.

Bob Butchart was much in favour, as the line went right past the end of his road—ideal for supplies and employee transportation. It would also bring many visitors to the Butchart estate.

Built at a cost of half a million dollars, the new track opened in June, 1913, just in time to witness an economic slump in the year leading up to the First World War. However, the line struggled through ten difficult years, with much of its business coming from tourist excursions to "Butchart's Gardens."

The second most expensive shelter (after the terminus station) was built at Tod Inlet for almost four hundred dollars, and there were fifteen return trips there every day, a scenic journey from downtown Victoria taking less than ninety minutes.

As automobiles and trucks became cheaper and more popular, however, freight traffic declined and the BCER's Saanich line closed in 1923, after carrying almost three million passengers.

The Italian Garden, during the late 1920s. The statue of Eros at the far end of the pond mysteriously disappeared.

THE ITALIAN GARDEN

This, the most formal garden on the estate, was created in 1926 after a suggestion made by Sir Henry Thornton, president of the Canadian National Railway, while he was visiting the Butcharts. Bob and Jenny had been to Italy several times, and were charmed by the idea, which also fit well with the Italian name of Benvenuto. Architect Samuel Maclure was involved in the design.

The old grass tennis court behind the house was dug up and a cross-shaped lily pond was sunk, utilizing a fountain of a girl and a dolphin which the Butcharts brought from Italy in 1924. This was surrounded by rectangular flower beds and large cement paving squares were laid to give a stately court-yard atmosphere. A bronze statue of Mercury the Messenger, brought from Florence by the Butcharts a year or so earlier,

61

The Star Pond — an elaborate playground for
Robert Butchart's exotic ducks.

was placed by the house to overlook the new garden, as he still
does today. This bright, sunny area soon became furnished
with chairs, benches and large umbrellas as a favourite haunt
for afternoon tea gatherings.

A *trelliage*, or gazebo, also designed by Maclure, was
built to the east side and until the bowling alley was added to
this wing of the residence a large chicken wire aviary housed
some of Bob's larger birds. The garden was separated from the
rest of the lawn to the north by a cypress hedge which today
towers above the garden.

Later, in the summer of 1928, the Star Pond was built,
designed by Seattle landscape architect Butler Sturtevant.
Originally this was simply called "the duck pond" and it was
a playground for Bob's ornamental ducks. It, too, had white
trellis work on its east side.

The pond was surrounded by a tall cryptomeria japon-
ica hedge, trained into archways almost 20 feet high, but a
severe frost in 1955 killed this, and it has never been replaced.
The outline is traced by a miniature English boxwood hedge
which dates back to before the Second World War.

The Italian Garden, the most formal area of the estate — but a most informal spot to entertain guests with afternoon tea.

By the late 1920s, industry was fading from the Butchart's property, though the old Fernie farmstead, unseen by the casual visitor, still had three jersey cows and a few of their offspring, some turkeys and a few chickens.

The kitchen garden and orchard still supplied the household with fresh produce, but flowers and seed had almost become the stock in trade for Bob and Jennie Butchart.

In fifteen years, Jennie had progressed from knowing almost nothing about gardening to being a celebrity in horticultural circles. She was in regular correspondence with major international seed producers and botanical gardens, and was frequently asked to judge at shows in Canada and the U.S.

BY LATE April, 1921, the last of the limestone had been quarried and carried down to the plant by conveyor belt and cable from the other side of Wallace Drive, a mile or so away. Quarrying couldn't go beyond the railway tracks and so the cement works that had provided work for hundreds of men over two decades began to quieten, and three towering smoke stacks loomed over the Sunken Garden like speechless sentinels.

The plant continued to make tiles, and flower pots in a characteristic grey colour were also produced. Some of these can be seen on display and in use at the Gardens today.

Cement production moved across the Saanich Inlet to Bamberton and plant workers commuted by boat every day. Bob had reached the traditional retirement age of sixty-five, but he was still active in various business interests, and deeply involved at home on the ripening estate.

By this time, Jennie had a regular gardening staff to help take care of the estate and since most of the heavy work had been done she no longer had to rely on help from Bob's labour force. Indeed, Jennie herself put many long days into the gar-

Dwarfed by cliffs in the Sunken Garden, a well-camouflaged gardener waters the rockery, circa 1921.

den, once working a full twelve hours the day after returning from a six month cruise.

One group of visitors while touring the estate came across a woman a shade over five feet tall, wearing a simple cotton dress, gumboots, and shielding her eyes from the sun with an old straw hat. Unknown to them, it was Jennie, dressed for practicality. She engaged them in conversation and was soon showing them her favourite parts of the acreage, pointing out little hideaways and vantage points to get the best views of the Sunken Garden.

Her knowledge of the plants was impressive, but what struck the visitors was her enthusiasm and obvious passion for her work. At the end of their private tour one of them offered her some "pin money" for her trouble.

"Oh no," she politely declined, "old Mrs. Butchart would never allow that."

This was Jennie at her most playful, living a role she played many times throughout her life. Over the years she would guide heads of state and royalty around her garden, but always with the same low-key charm and sincerity. When Rudyard Kipling said in his poem: "If you can talk with crowds and keep your virtue, or walk with Kings nor lose the common touch," he probably had Jennie's gift of grace in mind.

One of her favourite stories revolved around a high society dinner function, during which she sat next to the elderly Mrs. Prior, a lady of some refinement. Mrs. Prior asked how the Gardens were fertilized, and Jennie replied, candidly, that farmyard manure was the main nutrient. She added that, as far as quantities were concerned, it was obtained "by the yard."

"Good gracious," Mrs. Prior replied, "I hope you don't have it gift-wrapped!"

When asked by an impressed visitor how much the Gardens cost to keep in such immaculate condition, Jennie simply said: "I really don't know what this amounts to as I don't keep the books. I feel amply repaid, however, whatever the cost may be." The cost was, indeed, appreciable, with almost one hundred thousand dollars being spent on develop-

Jennie Butchart knits outside her summer house — a rare summer's day without a visitor in sight.

ment before 1920. But Bob's business acumen in the cement industry was no match for Jennie's gardening enthusiasm when it came to using the estate's acreage. "Each year I'm encroaching on Mr. Butchart's farm until the poor man's revenue from this source has entirely disappeared . . . I'm afraid the farm is doomed and a garden shall spring up in its place." How right she was. The vegetables would be chased away by roses and the orchard and kitchen garden would eventually become a concert lawn.

Occasionally, the Butchart home would open up to welcome certain visitors or distinguished groups, such as a "little party of zealous Sunday school teachers," or members of the British Association for the Advancement of Science. Jennie and Bob often joined their guests for refreshment, and perhaps to give an impromptu tour of the house. Once, however, when coming in from the garden and seeing a group of people about to take tea, Jennie politely asked if she could join them. Unaware of who she was they said no, and directed her to another table.

All set for croquet in the 1920s, with Jennie's largest teahouse in the background.

During the early 1920s the lawns behind the residence were given over to croquet and a sunken tennis court, surrounded by a wire fence. At the end of the upper lawn, near to where the Fountain of the Three Sturgeons is today, was a large summer house. Its walls and roof made of local Douglas fir with coarse bark, it housed grey wicker furniture, and a writing desk and table were provided for the use of guests. Various magazines were strewn around and long benches were gathered around the entrance.

Unfortunately, visitors were now so many in number that the Butcharts could no longer offer them free tea and other refreshments. Crockery was still provided and household staff would bring hot water so that visitors could make tea and eat their picnic lunches here, or beneath one of the many umbrellas that were available. However, people were inclined to take souvenirs to remember their visit, and the teapots, cups and spoons slowly disappeared.

It was not unusual, either, for people to take away a little more tangible proof that they'd been to Butchart Gardens. Bob Davis, a visiting journalist from New York City's *Evening Sun*, once asked Jennie how many people pick themselves a

The unofficial visitors' book — the teahouse roof in the Japanese Garden.

posy from the display beds. "Oh, my dear," Jennie replied, "they never even think of such a thing. If anyone felt like taking a flower from the Butchart gardens, Bob and I would be the last to object." Davis immediately helped himself to a rose. Jennie then took him to the seed store, undaunted by the fact that his "garden" consisted of a tiny window box on the eighth floor of a New York skyscraper, and gave him a packet of velvet pansy seeds.

Although "don't pick the flowers" signs have never appeared on the estate, one woman overstepped the mark. Jennie, noticing the woman's soiled hands and suspicious behaviour as she hurried towards the gate, politely asked her to return the stolen goods. "Please, if you don't mind, I'd like my plants to stay in my garden." And the woman meekly handed over a shopping bag full of rare alpine plants that Jennie and Bob had recently brought back from foreign travels.

The Gardens, ever popular with lovers as they are today, were also subject to a little abuse from knife-wielding suitors, anxious to leave their precious mark on trees. In an effort to prevent this practice getting out of hand Bob erected a small sign at a one silver poplar tree which said: "carve initials here."

That tree has now gone but the practice of graffiti continues down in the Japanese garden. The underside of the roof of both pagodas bear a myriad inscriptions, in chalk, ball-point, pencil and various hues of lipstick. Even when the roofs of these small buildings are renewed the multi-lingual writing beneath it stays intact.

Another item that caused concern, and still does, is the taking of seeds or cuttings by visitors. Gardeners from around the world have discreetly, and overtly, helped themselves to a few seed pods, or a twig they hope to propagate when they get home. Acknowledging this, the Gardens have made packaged seeds available to visitors for almost 80 years.

SEEDS FOR SALE

Jennie set aside four and a half acres, on either side of the road leading to the residence, solely for growing seed stock. Early requests, often made directly to the gardeners, were informally filled. Any money made from seed sales was put into a general fund and shared out among the gardening staff as an annual bonus.

When Archie Nicholls was head gardener he had more than one administrative skirmish with Bob when it came to seeds. They would generally agree on what stock was needed for the upcoming year's planting, and order it from nurseries

Jennie Butchart in the gateway to her private garden, November, 1928.

*There is a garden
in her face
Where roses
and white lilies grow*

THOMAS CAMPION
(1567-1620)

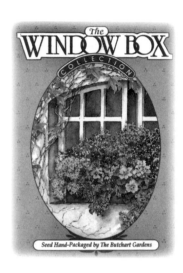

Seeds from Butchart Gardens have been on sale since 1920. A mail order business soon grew, supplying photographs, videotapes and garden tools.

in the UK. What they didn't seem to know, and didn't always agree on, was which of them was going to send out the order. They often ended up with twice as much stock as was needed, much to Bob's annoyance.

The Benvenuto Seed Company started officially in 1920 and seeds of all kinds were offered, together with sowing instructions and tips for successful propagation.

Jennie became passionate about this new enterprise, kept a close watch on expenses and set out to demonstrate that it could be profitable. (Benvenuto itself certainly wasn't, its maintenance and hosting of visitors costing the Butcharts almost ten thousand dollars a year at this time). But Jennie proclaimed that "seed-growing is an occupation that lies ready for women who wish to earn their living in connection with the land."

In 1923, the inventory had two hundred and four seed types listed, with twenty-four varieties of sweet pea alone. Two years later a new seed store had to be built.

By 1951, catalogue number twenty-four ran to over thirty pages with seed varieties in the hundreds, from aconitum to zinnia. This growing mail-order business could also supply hand-coloured photographs of the Gardens or 35mm slides, and fifty-five cents would buy one of the popular Viewmaster reels with seven three-dimensional Kodachrome views.

During the mid-1980s the Flower Seed Postcard was introduced, a seed pack measuring four and a half inches by six, which could be stamped, addressed and mailed anywhere in the world.

In 1996, the catalogue was published as a full-colour brochure and in addition to seeds and six packaged seed collections for rock gardens, window boxes, and cottage gardens (as well as one designed for children), aluminum hand tools were being offered. And a twenty-two minute video with an original music score and narration has replaced the Viewmaster series. It also contains some black and white footage of the early years at Benvenuto, with Jennie serving tea to visitors.

Apart from collecting seeds during trips around the world, Jennie would also correspond with gardens and nurseries to acquire new stock.

The age of horticultural exploration, though in its peak some years earlier during the reign of Queen Victoria, was still in vogue. Explorers would go off in search of new flora, sometimes returning empty-handed or having been beaten to the prize. Occasionally, the botanical bounty hunter wouldn't return at all.

PLANT EXPLORATION

The Butcharts worked hard and travelled far to improve their collection of plants on the estate, despite the trouble it must have been—keeping a young sapling alive while transporting it around the world is difficult enough today, in the air cargo era of climate control and refrigeration. Until old age curtailed their freedom somewhat, Bob and Jennie spent about half of every year away from Benvenuto, always returning with new specimens, statuary, or a new idea to incorporate into their landscape.

Canada has had horticultural regulations and laws since 1805, when an act was passed to preserve apple trees in Montreal. Two federal acts, in 1898 and 1910 controlled Destructive Insects and Pests, but soil or plant importation laws were certainly not as strict as they are today, so the Butcharts, and others, made the most of it.

At a general meeting of the Victoria Natural History Society, held in May 1914, a letter from a Mr. H. L. Salmon, about to leave on a trip to England, was read, generously offering to: "obtain seeds or plants of indigenous English plants for distribution in Vancouver Island." It wasn't too difficult in those days to drive across a Canadian border with a bag of seed, or a plant in a bucket of soil. Suffice to say that on June 7, 1921, the Western Plant Quarantine Board, with representatives from ten of the United States and British Columbia, toured the Gardens, apparently without interrogating the estate's owners.

The Butcharts would gather flora in the Himalayas and the Pyrenees, and were the first people to drive from the Cape of Africa to Cairo, collecting specimens as they went. Road trips to the southern U.S. and Mexico were always fruitful, and

Bob and Jennie Butchart outside the largest of the Gardens' teahouses, made out of slabwood Douglas fir.

the task, they knew, was endless. They were extending a trail that had been blazed for years by explorers, seeking trophies that future generations of gardeners would appreciate, and possibly take for granted as nursery inventories were expanded.

In 1879, after following the Ygantze River upstream for many miles, explorer Charles Maries reported that all Chinese species of any use had already been introduced. And this opinion was widely accepted for over twenty years. Later, in 1899, when Earnest Wilson was dispatched from the Veitch Nursery of England to find the fabled "Handkerchief tree" (*Davidia involucrata*), his boss said: "Stick to the one thing that you are after, and do not spend time or money wandering about. Probably almost every worthwhile plant in China has now been introduced."

Fortunately, Wilson didn't follow instructions too closely, and after eleven years of wandering about Asia he introduced well over a thousand new plants, which changed the face of Western gardens. And the Butchart estate has three "Handkerchief" trees which bloom every May.

Over a century later, many people still feel that any worthy temperate garden plant has already been collected and tested, but in *Fang*, Wen-Pei's notable 1981 work on Chinese maples, he acknowledges one hundred and forty-three species. Today, only six of these are easily found North American nurseries, with maybe a dozen or so more in botanic garden collections, amounting to a mere fraction of the known total. No doubt a few "undiscovered" specimens are still lurking in remote areas of China.

The most famous Butchart tale of plant exploration concerns Captain Frederick Marshman Bailey, a British Army officer and explorer. He was visiting the Gardens and being quite impressed by the floral displays and exotic bird species which Jennie and Bob had gathered. Over lunch, however, Captain Bailey made a friendly bet with Jennie that she didn't have a plant that he'd proudly retrieved on a recent expedition: "the Blue Poppy of Tibet."

She graciously accepted the wager, and after lunch took him down to the Japanese Garden where a fine example of this perennial flower was in full bloom. The captain regained a little composure, if not his bet, when Jennie told him the seeds had come from a friend of hers at the Edinburgh Botanical Garden, where Bailey had sent his original specimen. Bailey was awarded a gold medal from the Royal Geographical Society for his discovery of this flower, *Meconopsis* , which has grown in the Gardens since the 1920s. Seeds for it are still on sale in the gift shop today.

The Butchart estate and Tod Inlet seen from the air in 1927. The unpaved road leads down to the old cement works and the entrance lane to the house is dotted with hawthorn trees. The new Italian Garden can be seen behind the house while beyond the kitchen garden and orchard are the old farm buildings – now the site of the concert lawn and fireworks viewing area.

THE ROAD TO BUTCHART'S

A map dated 1895 shows Lime Kiln Road heading down towards Tod Inlet, stopping short some quarter of a mile from the waterfront. Until Bob developed the cement works it

"That which we call a rose, by any other name would smell as sweet." — William Shakespeare

I n an effort to maintain the charm and appearance of a private garden, most plants on the estate are left unlabeled, as they were in Jennie Butchart's time, (unless they have special historical interest or some other notable feature). Benvenuto is a show garden, aiming to please and entertain, as opposed to a purely botanical garden which provides detailed information, sometimes as a compromise to appearances. Labels also tend to invite people off the footpaths and into the flower beds for a closer look. The rose garden is the only place on the estate where name plates are prevalent. These used to be small tags on short wooden posts but have been replaced by white plastic labels mounted on black metal stakes, which blend in surprisingly, despite their number.

Many roses are named after celebrities and show the country and year of origin, such as:

BING CROSBY U.S.A. 1981
INGRID BERGMAN DENMARK 1984
DOLLY PARTON U.S.A. 1983
CARY GRANT FRANCE 1987
Politics are represented:
MR. LINCOLN U.S.A. 1964
BARBARA BUSH
Some rose labels offer a surprising combination of name and country:
EIFFEL TOWER U.S.A. 1963
LAS VEGAS GERMANY 1981
And some hint at trans-Atlantic coincidence:
IVORY TOWER GERMANY 1979
IVORY TOWER U.S.A. 1979

was little more than a rough, dirt road, making its way down from two hundred and fifty feet above sea-level. The road descended to the village at Tod Inlet, with an abrupt turn off leading to the Butchart residence, either side of which were planted hawthorn trees. (This would remain the entrance and exit to Benvenuto until traffic problems in the early 1950s forced the building of a new entrance road, the one used today. Visitors still leave the Gardens along the hawthorn avenue).

The single track was pitted with deep holes; muddy puddles in winter and dust bowls in summer. Most cement works traffic came and went by water, as did many of the Gardens visitors, so at first there was little pressure to pave the road. When the railway started depositing goods, and visitors, the traffic increased and it soon became clear that a good road was needed.

Bob offered a labour force and crushed rock from his quarry, and the municipality came up with a thousand dollars to supply a steam roller and thick oil to bind the fill together, and keep down the dust.

However, as traffic increased the road took a beating and soon it was almost impassable. It got so bad in the spring of 1927 that the Saanich Board of Trade voted unanimously on a resolution "that as long as Limekiln Road is in its present condition that Mr. Butchart be asked to close his gardens."

Temporary repairs were made and the Gardens remained open, and Bob set about plans to pave the road properly, with cement. Ironically, two weeks later, Bob found out only too well how dangerous a poorly-kept road can be. Driving through Woodland, California, on the way back from Los Angeles, he skidded on loose sand and overturned the car. He and Jennie were taken to Woodland hospital with serious injuries.

Up until the 1920s, concrete had not been used for road paving in this part of the world, but as soon as it was, Bob was keen to show it off. The first section of local road to get the "concrete for permanence" treatment was a stretch of the Island Highway running through Colwood, about twenty miles away, close to where Bob played golf occasionally.

He sent a letter to the Saanich council, inviting them to come and drive over the new road, to see how smooth it was. A reply, dated July 9, 1920, accepted the offer and all were suitably impressed. A stretch of the West Saanich Road was also paved in concrete, and as good and durable as it was, the cost was too much to do all municipal roads this way. Motorized traffic, though, was certainly on the increase.

By 1927, some three hundred and fifty thousand visitors were coming to Victoria each year, driving over eighteen thousand automobiles. Those who ventured up the peninsula and followed the signs to Tod Inlet and Butchart's Gardens had a slow, rough ride, despite a local hotel's travel brochure which advertised "beautiful country roads reminiscent of Merrie England."

Finally, at midnight on Sunday, March 29 1929, Lime Kiln Road was closed to all vehicular traffic while it too was paved. Ironically, the cement had to come from across the water at Bamberton, as Tod Inlet works had long since stopped producing. A story persists that the paving was a rushed job, in preparation for a visit to the Gardens by Queen Marie of Romania. Unfortunately, the queen changed her travel plans and the visit was never made.

Most of 1929 was cool and wet, and hardly the weather for touring a garden. The late spring also brought with it a record-breaking tent caterpillar season that almost devastated local fruit farms and took a toll on the Butchart's trees. This didn't deter admiring visitors, who could now rent a car downtown for a couple of dollars and drive out to Tod Inlet for the day. By early August that year they were finally rewarded with some hot, dry weather, perfect for a garden picnic.

Just before Christmas that same year, the name Lime Kiln Road was dropped and Benvenuto officially took its place in the British Columbia Gazette as a primary highway. Today, it's the only one of the three original concrete roads still visible, the others having been replaced long ago.

Heavy tour buses and delivery trucks have taken their toll and many of the slabs have cracked and had to be patched, quite crudely in places, with black asphalt. The original Benvenuto Avenue was barely wide enough to handle the traffic of 1930 and

Not long before he died, Robert Butchart had a lake named after him.

Butchart Lake sits at 48°32 North and 123°39 West, just a few miles to the west of Benvenuto, and forms part of the Goldstream watershed in the Greater Victoria Water District.

It was formed during the 1890s and is now contained by one of the major dams in the province of British Columbia.

today large vehicles must take extra caution, especially during icy conditions.

Visitors arriving by car at the Gardens during the 1920s didn't present much of a parking problem, and a grassy area where the toll booths are today was usually big enough to accommodate them. On one occasion, however, a certain vehicle gave cause for some concern.

Bob and Jennie returned to Benvenuto late one night from an appointment downtown to find a strange car parked in their driveway. Visitors were supposed to leave at dusk and Jennie was annoyed that someone had stayed so late. She immediately sent Bob off around the gardens with a flashlight to find the culprit, while she prepared to teach the laggard a lesson in manners.

He came back almost an hour later, after an exhaustive search, and assured her there was no one left on the estate. They retired to bed.

Early next morning they were awoken by a commotion outside on the driveway. Members of the staff were gathered around the offending vehicle talking excitedly, one of them speaking in less than hushed tones. Every tire on the car was flat.

Unfortunately, Jennie's lesson in manners went not to a tardy visitor, but to her own gardener who'd only just got the car. She kept her little mistake a closely guarded secret for years, sharing it only with her closest friends.

BOB GETS FREEDOM OF THE CITY

Already a highly respected businessman and industrial leader, Bob Butchart garnered many awards from all kinds of organizations. In September 1927 he was made the first ever Honorary Kinsman by the local Victoria chapter and was presented with a gold pin.

Less than a year later, at the age of seventy-two, he was to receive the highest honor of his career. The Freedom of the City of Victoria had been awarded only once before, to Lord Willingdon, who was made a free citizen of the provincial capital because of his role as messenger of the King.

The ceremony took place at Victoria City Hall, at 11 a.m. on the morning of Friday, June 22, 1928. In a chamber specially decorated in the city's colours of white and blue, 150 invited guests repeatedly interrupted the proceedings with spontaneous applause for Bob and Jennie. Bob received a parchment scroll detailing the formal resolution from council and a silver casket containing the symbolic golden key. Victoria mayor, J. C. Penray, addressed Bob on behalf of Greater Victoria and brought laughter from the crowd when he said: "You, sir, have the pleasure of knowing that you are the first man who has ever made the councils of Victoria, Esquimalt, Oak Bay and Saanich absolutely unanimous on any one question."

Bob was visibly moved by the occasion, and his reply included the words "We have looked for years on the Saanich Peninsula as one of the most beautiful places in the world, and we have tried in our modest way to keep it so. May I assure you of our devotion to the city of Victoria and to the prosperity of the City and its surrounding municipalities . . . we are overcome by your kindness and ask you to accept our appre-

Jennie Butchart —"Our Colonel"
of the Victoria Girls Drill Team,
c. 1940.

ciation from the bottom of our hearts."

Jennie was also honored and presented with a silver tea
tray bearing the city's crest and inscribed: *"Presented to Mrs.
R. P. Butchart by the citizens of Victoria and district in appreciation of her public services. June 22, 1928."*

Despite the enormity of the ceremony, Jennie was true
to her spirit and replied with good humour: "All I can say is to
thank you for your very great kindness to us. I had a little
speech all prepared, but Mr. Butchart insisted on waking me
up in the middle of the night. He was worrying about what he

would say. 'What shall I say, Jennie?' he kept asking me, and I have forgotten everything I would have said. I was certainly tired when I awoke and prepared to come to the ceremony only to find an escort of police outside waiting for us. I was surprised, for the only other occasion I remember having a police escort was when we were being taken before the judge in California for violating some traffic regulation.

We are so happy to be here with you all, and you have been so good to us. This afternoon, about four o'clock, we are going to be at home at Benvenuto and we would be happy to see you all, all who are here and all who are not, out there for tea. Bring your wives and sweethearts and come and have tea with us, and see the beautiful flowers, they are so pretty at this time of year."

And although the weather that day was cloudy and cool, they had a good turnout.

It was one of the very few occasions that the Gardens were closed to the general public.

A week later, Bob sent a handwritten letter to council, thanking them for bestowing the honor, and adding: "The beautiful silver casket and tray and the illuminated address will be treasured by my wife and myself as our greatest possession." It certainly was, and it took pride of place in the Butchart's dining room at Benvenuto.

JENNIE'S PRIVATE GARDEN

By the early 1920s, Bob and Jennie were hosting some five or six hundred visitors every day during spring and summer, and generally loved the company. They often remarked, in fact, how lonely it seemed later in the year when the last of

Jennie Butchart's private garden — sanctuary for the lady of the house. A step simply marked "Private" kept most of her curious visitors out.

the rose petals had fallen and visitors became fewer in number.

In September, 1920, Samuel Maclure drafted a design for a twenty-five foot long private tea house for Jennie, just to the west of the main residence. The interior was decorated in pale blue and a china cabinet in a corner held an array of delicate cups and saucers. Boxes and hanging baskets of pink geraniums and draconas completed the picture. The cosy room looked back towards the house, over a tidy green lawn and a small, formal pond, filled with water lilies and supplied with tinkling water from a fish held by a small cherub. This was surrounded by blue irises, misty blue ageratum, heliotrope and yet more pink geraniums.

The garden was tastefully enclosed using white lattice-work fencing, barely wider than the tearoom and bowered with climbing roses. A white gateway led in from the court-

The son of a Royal Engineer, Samuel Maclure was the first non-native child to be born in New Westminster, then the largest city in the province in 1860. After training as a telegraph operator, he spent a year studying at Spring Garden Art School in Philadelphia, and moved to Victoria in 1892 to become one of its most famous architects. He shared an office at 606 Fort Street with Francis Rattenbury, the man who designed the British Columbia Legislature.

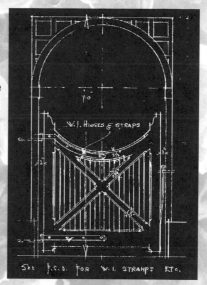

Fresh from his renowned work at the lavish Hatley Park castle west of Victoria, Maclure worked as architectural consultant for Bob and Jennie Butchart from 1911 to 1925, carrying out extensive renovations to their home and designing several features of the estate.

Maclure was an avid gardener, and would go to great lengths to site a dwelling to avoid removing trees or altering terrain. He often worked and learned much of his art, apparently, from reference books, particularly one by the late-eighteenth century landscaper, William Robinson. He also introduced Bob and Jennie to the Robillard family of landscape gardeners, who had worked extensively for Maclure's affluent Rockland area clients. (The Robillards would soon come to work at the Gardens and they, too, would leave a distinguishing mark).

Maclure was also an outspoken naturalist, and wrote to the Victoria *Daily Colonist* in June 1922 to criticize the city's pruning of trees. He gained the support of several experts of the time in his effort to ". . . do something to prevent the abominable orchardizing of the city trees."

There were allegations that his Hatley Park castle design was copied from the country home of the Duchess of Warwick, but Maclure prided himself on originality. The house he built for Jennie's daughter Mary, at 944 St. Charles Street, introduced to Victoria the "battered" rough cast stucco, the pantiled roof, and unusual *porte-cochere*, or carriage entrance. In 1927, almost at the end of his career, he was asked to design the gardens for Government House in Victoria, which he'd worked on as co-architect.

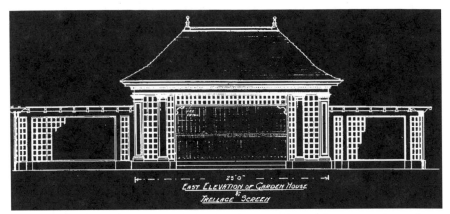

The original design for Jennie Butchart's private garden tea house, as drawn by Samuel Maclure in September, 1920.

yard and across twenty-one little flagstone steps to another gateway opposite. The flagstone at the threshold was engraved with the word "Private," and for the most part, the word was obeyed.

Jennie enjoyed some degree of privacy in this little green haven but would occasionally invite people in to join her. Ferns and palms were planted in the bed beneath the house windows and before the Italian Garden was built, this was the most formal, or "finished" area of the estate.

This private garden has remained virtually unchanged for almost eighty years. Gardens staff still speak about it with reverence and rarely is anyone seen within its confines. Today, a cast iron table and four chairs sit vacantly in the tea house, as if awaiting Jennie Butchart's return.

Weeding the Sunken Garden lake takes time and caution - it's fifty feet deep in places, hence the life-vest.

The last of Tod Inlet village - a derelict cow barn.

Blue Poppies - still special after more than seventy years.

"A cloud above the depth pro-found" - the Sunken Garden lake.

A dash of wildflower colour in the old cement works.

A Butchart Gardens' sequoia enjoys tender, loving care, and one of the best tree-growing climates in North America.

Winter solitude in the Japanese Garden.

The teahouse - a peaceful legacy of the Zen Buddhist garden from several centuries ago.

The "eternal beauty of evergreens" gave the tea ceremony its due focus.

Once a tennis court, now the Italian Garden.

An upstairs bowling alley forms the east wing of the garden, and shelters the gallery of visitors' books.

A bronze statue of Mercury, brought from Florence by the Butcharts, has enjoyed this view for more than seventy years.

The Italian Garden fountain, brought from Italy by Robert and Jennie
Butchart in 1924 - two years later it had its own pond.

The lake, where Bob summoned
trout by clapping his hands.

Once fenced off for safety, the
deepest quarry now sparkles.

A quiet corner of the prettiest
parking lot in the province.

The oldest part of the Sunken
Garden, from the lookout cabin.

THE ROSE GARDEN

JENNIE'S FIRST gardening venture began with just a few Caroline Testout roses, obtained soon after she came to Tod Inlet, but it set her on a course to showcase this most romantic of flowers.

The patch of land just west of the residence, which was to become the Rose Garden, had at first been home to a few vegetables, creatively screened by tall perennials, hollyhocks and delphiniums in Jennie's favourite blue. Several archways, twenty feet apart and smothered by climbing roses, led the visitor along a grassy path to a sundial mounted on a red brick plinth, inscribed "A.D. 1706 Sunny Days."

In 1929 Jennie commissioned designs to formalize the garden from Butler S. Sturtevant, a Seattle landscape consultant, and put her new head gardener, Bob Ballantyne to the task. The simple rectangular shape of the old patch was given grace and stature by an oval lawn, accented with a fountain and wrought iron wishing well, surrounded by rose beds, and leading off through a long archway covered with roses.

The Rose Garden before its formal landscaping — vegetables vie for position.

By 1995, over six and a half thousand roses were being grown, including one hundred and fifty varieties of hybrid tea and floribunda rose. The roses include sweet-smelling old varieties, like the "Felicite et Perpetue" which dates back to 1827, before the Butchart ancestors came to Canada. Others, such as "Edith Cavell," are from the 1930s when Jennie was still actively looking for new plants. Prize-winning specimens from all over the world are still being added to the Rose Garden today.

Some of the climbing roses cling to wooden poles and some are trained around concrete archwork, sculpted and cast to look like the bark-covered limbs of a tree. This practice began when Bob Butchart, concerned at the lack of Garry oak trees on the estate, had oak "branches" made from cement to decorate the gardens and provide a framework for climbing plants. A cement artist called Frank Scolli, from Monte Carlo, made at least one of the large cement tree stumps still on view today and further examples of cement sculpture are seen all around the Rose Garden and the Japanese Garden. Small

"Sunny Days" - The sundial was already over 200 years old when the formal Rose Garden was landscaped in 1929.

cement pillars holding sand-filled ash trays are dotted around the estate and the handrail for the steps leading up to the Star Pond from the north side shows some of the original sculpting and some, more crudely fashioned, has been added over the years.

As 1930 drew to a close, bad news reached the home of Benvenuto. Bob and Jennie's son-in-law, Harry Allan Ross, had been ill for some time and died on Friday November 7, 1930 at the age of fifty-two. Harry's wife, Jenny, was with him at their home on Runnymede Avenue and a funeral was held there the following day. Harry was survived by his son, Robert Ian, then a boy of twelve, but who became the owner of Butchart Gardens a few years down the road. Ian lived at

Benvenuto for a time when he was young, and began his career there working occasionally as a parking attendant, at the tender age of five years old. It was a job he enjoyed and returned to for the next seventy years or so.

Grandchildren and visiting children now figured largely at Benvenuto, and Jennie made sure they were welcome, and entertained. There were swings, slides and sand piles available, and two little Shetland ponies were ready to ride, or to pull youngsters around in a Sicilian pony cart. The children even had their own tiny little chairs and tables under shady maple trees.

And in those days, the Gardens were home to a host of other little people, especially in the Japanese Garden. Tiny garden gnomes invited a pat from inquisitive children, surprised to feel the little porcelain faces so cold to the touch. Cheeky little fairies and brownies peeked out from behind foliage, or sat at the edge of a pond, fishing rods in hand.

Here's how one writer described her encounter with them in 1920: *"One saucy brownie rocks himself in a swing suspended from the crotch of a dwarf tree, his cheery grin an everlasting challenge to all sombre thoughts. Gnomes without number sit in meditative silence on the cool grass or on stumps, keeping watchful eyes on passers-by. A quaint little brownie with a philosophical cast of countenance, serenely smokes an old-fashioned Dutch pipe, while a little farther on a more waggish member of the family drinks eternally out of an empty stein with an air of perfect relish."*

Three little fishermen gnomes, sitting on a rock behind the snail fountain near the gift shop side entrance, survived until the late 1970s.

The enclosed verandah in Benvenuto. The library is immediately to the right while the door straight ahead leads into the billiard room and beyond it the indoor swimming pool. The north-facing windows looked out over the old tennis court, which was soon to become the Italian Garden.

BENVENUTO, THE HOME

Even at the age of sixty-four, Jennie would often be seen working cheerfully in the garden, cutting flowers for the house or culling flowers that were past their best. By now, her home was attracting fifty thousand visitors a year, and she'd inevitably be mistaken for an employee. One fine day a lady approached Jennie, who was examining some new addition to the Rose Garden, and struck up a candid conversation, saying: "Do you work here?" Jennie admitted that she did and was immediately asked "What wages do you get?"

The first architectural drawing of the whole house, completed in 1922 by Samuel Maclure. The upstairs swimming pool was the builder's biggest challenge.

"I can't complain," replied Jennie, "I'm satisfied."

"Oh," continued the woman, indicating the residence, "I guess they must be worth all of a million, eh?"

"I shouldn't like to ask that."

"Well," said the woman, turning to march away, "all I can say is that they've got a queer patched-up house for millionaires!"

Cheeky as it was, the comment had an element of truth, since the residence had never been designed or built as a whole. Benvenuto rambles and spreads, and is much larger inside than most people would think. Its shape and design have largely been the work of one man: Samuel Maclure. "We built on a room here and there whenever we wanted it," Jennie would say later, when asked about the unusual layout of her home.

Samuel Maclure may have been the original builder of the first house on the estate, and he was certainly commissioned to make various renovations to the home and gardens over a twelve year period. In 1911 he began by designing a sun room for the home, followed by drawings for some custom-built furniture, including a serving table.

Another major renovation was the two-storey addition, which Bob required for a garage, billiard room and indoor swimming pool. The swimming pool posed an architectural challenge, and one that was met, not surprisingly, by using lots of cement and concrete. Access to the pool was upstairs, so on the ground floor, next to the garage, huge pillars were built to take the weight. The tank was lined with ceramic tiles, bordered with mauve, green and black squares, and salt water was pumped up from the inlet, twinkling below sunshine which flooded through a large skylight overhead.

The main drawing room, decorated in "old rose," led through wide doors to a large conservatory, built in 1917, with a splashing wall fountain and rich green banks of palms, ferns and begonias. A private roof garden was also added that year.

Maclure altered the library, making it warmly inviting in burnt orange and black, and featuring a Japanese temple table and a rare pair of exquisite table seats in brown lacquer. The billiard room, too, was richly decorated in mulberry brocade and black walnut, and featured a large table imported from the British firm of Burroughes and Watts. This area would later house the incredible Paganini Violin-Piano which Bob picked up at the Leipzig Trade Fair in 1928. (This latest piece of musical engineering could be played manually or automatically by paper rolls).

The sun room was remodelled in 1919 to incorporate classical decor, and Maclure's attention to detail is displayed in the dining room, decorated in blue and ivory, and commanding a spectacular view over the main lawn down to Butchart Cove. An indoor bowling alley was built in the upstairs wing which overlooks the Italian Garden. Bob's love of things nau-

God gave the earth to glorify,
Green field and wooded hill
But I would render thanks to those
Who made earth fairer still

And lest man might forget the stars
That shine the night away
God made the flowers, starry-eyed
To shine for Him by day

When God made other living things
He thought of magic words
That men might never learn to speak
And taught them to the birds

And when God thought to make of man
Of all His works the warden
He tuned his soul to beauty's note
And set him in a garden

So this is proof that they are Kings
And Queens by ancient right
Who clothe earth's nakedness and scars
With garments of delight

Dr. H.J.T. Coleman, a former dean of arts at the University of British Columbia, was so moved during a visit to Benvenuto in the 1920s that he penned this poem, as a tribute to the Butcharts.

104

tical also made its way into the home, and the staircase leading to the Aeolian pipe organ loft reportedly came from an old
sailing ship. Another area of the house, known as the Tango
Room, is supposed to be panelled with wood from some
ancient yacht. (An English company, based in Northumberland,
later supplied the estate with benches made of teak that was
salvaged from old British sailing ships. One such bench occurs
along the pathway leading from the Rose Garden to the
Fountain of the Three Sturgeons, and can seat about twelve
people).

In 1922, possibly with grandchildren in mind, the
Butcharts added two attic bedrooms at the west end of the
house and an extra bathroom to the south side. It was during
this period that the first overall plan of Benvenuto was cap-
tured on paper, as Maclure drew detailed sketches of all three
storeys.

The architect's work is also evident outside the home.
A two-room seed store and greenhouse were built in the early
1920s, plus extensive *trelliage*, a private garden and tea house
for Jennie, and an elaborate hillside house for Bob's ducks. He
also designed the "Chinaman's Cottage" in 1917, which still
stands at the end of the seed gardens where the hawthorn-lined
exit road joins Benvenuto Avenue.

JENNIE IS VICTORIA'S "BEST CITIZEN" IN 1931

Their regular travels, often by car, had introduced the
Butcharts to many people up and down the west coast, and
word of their fabulous gardens had travelled even further.
They were revered and celebrated wherever they went, and
despite Bob's success and international reputation as a leading

industrialist, his wife's renown as a gardener gave her equal billing.

The citizens of Wenatchee, Washington State, had honored them in mid-July of 1931, for their "outstanding public benefactions in making the world a little brighter for uncounted thousands of individuals." And then, on Monday night, July 20, 1931 Jennie was invited downtown to The Empress Hotel to help the Native Sons and Native Daughters of British Columbia celebrate the diamond jubilee of Canadian Confederation. But the main celebration of the evening was to be Jennie herself.

Every year, a panel of Victoria citizens, sponsored by the Sons and Daughters, selected a person worthy of being named Best Citizen for the year. Jennie was formally introduced to the distinguished guests by Mayor Herbert Anscomb as "the lady of Benvenuto." He went on to say: "This honor is an expression by the people of the love they have for this great citizen, Mrs. Butchart."

The assembled guests, including many foreign visitors, rose with loud cheering and applause, and Jennie was cheerfully toasted by Mr. R. Hiscocks, the chief factor of the Native Sons.

With typical modesty, Jennie thanked the assembly warmly for the honor, and then said: "I do not feel that I have done anything to merit this great distinction.

It has always been a pleasure for me to try and cultivate, and it has given me joy to share our home and garden with others. I accept this honor and share it with Mr. Butchart.

I trust that Benvenuto, the name of our home and garden, will ever convey the meaning of Welcome to the citizens of Victoria. Thank you."

Letters of congratulation flooded in, from individuals, organizations and municipalities, and in many cases Jennie replied to them in her own hand, such as in the following letter to Saanich council:

Tod Inlet BC
July 25th 1931

Dear Mr. Sewell,

Your nice letter received. It is so kind of the Municipal Council to write me congratulation. I am delighted with the honor and hope I may be able to live up to it. Victorians have been most kind to us and anything we can do to show our appreciation will always be a pleasure.
Thanking you
Yours sincerely
Jennie Butchart

The *Colonist* said: "There is no lady in this quarter of the Empire better known throughout the continent than Mrs. Butchart." To which the *Times* added: "The gardens at Benvenuto do more than appeal to lovers of floral beauty. They form an arresting demonstration of the fertility of our soil and the kindliness of our climate . . . they have been the most effective advertisement Greater Victoria has had."

It was an advertisement that worked. Journalists from New York were describing Benvenuto as "the finest private garden in the Dominion of Canada, if not in the whole of North America." People were now coming in droves to see the Gardens.

Although boats of all sizes still plied the quiet waters of the inlet bringing hundreds to walk up through the Japanese Garden, Bob's new cement road meant easy access for motor vehicles. Sundays were so busy that local police had to control

The Butcharts cultivated the tour bus industry as quickly as they grew flowers — a weekly bus in the 1920s became over a hundred a day by the 1990s.

traffic at the main gate, and the Butcharts were helping to fuel a whole new industry: tour buses.

TO BENVENUTO BY BUS

During the 1920s, renting an automobile became affordable to a middle-income couple, or a group of friends looking for a weekend excursion, and the driver's licence was still a thing of the future. Automobiles got larger and a few entrepreneurs saw the potential in taking a half-dozen or more sightseers out of the city for a spin. Butchart Gardens seemed a natural destination, being within easy reach of Victoria and asking no admission price.

Four-seater cars gave way to six-seaters which led to the touring car and the jitney, followed in due course by the motor coach which could carry around thirty passengers. C & C (Cameron & Calwell) Transportation had a depot at 906 Government Street and their blue and white open-topped buses were a familiar sight around Victoria. They were among the first operators to take visitor groups out to Benvenuto. Island Coach Lines was formed by Harold Husband in 1928 and seeing the increase in tourist trade, he shrewdly picked up a Gray Line franchise to become a fully-fledged tour operator

George "Rebel" Mowat (to the right in cap) was the Gardens' most famous tour guide. On this June afternoon in 1935 he shows a party of Puget Sound Travel Directors around the Rose Garden. As raconteur he was surpassed only by his friend, Jennie Butchart. As horticulturalist he was often quite inventive, but never stumped for an answer.

and, eventually, the largest bus operator in the region.

An article in a 1952 Maclean's magazine said that the Gardens bus tours "spawned a new school of showmen, the fast-talking never-stuck-for-an-answer sight-seeing guides." One such guide had been taking visitors to Benvenuto for years, and was already a local legend, and friend of Jennie Butchart. His name was George, or "Rebel" Mowat, a Brooklyn native who drove a Courier 86 bus for Gray Line. He would pick up passengers in front of The Empress Hotel and take them on a three-hour return trip out to the Gardens, with commentary every inch of the way. Rebel told a local reporter his hobbies were "talking, talking, talking, and tropical fish," and his passengers could testify to this. Whatever the question, he was never at a loss for words and often gave out dubious horticultural information.

Once, when taking a tour group across the courtyard in front of the house he encountered Gardens' staff installing a brand new cement statue. "Who's that?" asked one of his group, and, even though he'd never seen the figure before, Rebel said "Chief Malahat." The statue is still informally known by that name today.

Jennie, of course, took an affectionate shine to him and would occasionally sneak aboard Rebel's bus in Victoria to get a lift back home to Benvenuto, sitting anonymously among his fare-paying passengers.

Rebel and other drivers, whom Jennie called "my boys," were often invited into the Butchart home for tea, or to shelter from inclement weather. Accomplished as they were at story-telling, Jennie would more than match the tour guides with her sense of humour and skill as raconteur.

One American visitor fell into a pool in the Sunken Garden while Rebel was there. Jennie rushed over to comfort the unfortunate soul, and took her into the house to dry off. The gracious hostess of Benvenuto went out of her way to ensure the woman was made comfortable and loaned her dry clothes, sending the wet ones via her chauffeur-driven car down into Victoria for dry cleaning. They were delivered as soon as possible to the visitor's hotel. On her return home to Seattle, the woman sued Jenny for damages.

It was Rebel Mowat, apparently, who had the idea for the wishing well in the Rose Garden. Every week he would plunge in with high rubber boots to collect coins from the watery coffers, carting them back to the house in a wheelbarrow to be packed off to some charitable cause.

The British double-decker - a regular
sight here since the 1960s.

In the 1960s the now-famous red double-decker bus
made its first appearance on Victoria's streets, and thirty years
later Gray Line had a fleet of more than fifty of them shuttling
tourists up to the Gardens, seventy-two at a time. (Almost half
of Gray Line's business comes from Gardens tours and the firm
now averages sixty trips a day during summer months).

In 1945, a trip out to Benvenuto on Vancouver Island
Coach Lines cost fifty cents for a one-way fare, or ninety cents
return. In the 1990s a similar, though more luxurious trip costs
around thirty dollars, depending on the time of year. (This

price includes the Gardens' entrance fee, which varies according to the season).

BC Transit started to provide a service from downtown Victoria to the Gardens in 1987, a fifty-minute journey which also carried many commuters, stopping at various points en route. The last bus returning to the city is usually late enough for nighttime visitors, and will often wait for them on Saturday evenings in July and August, when the fireworks show is on. In 1989 this service was taking about eighteen hundred passengers a week to the Gardens and just four years later the figure had almost doubled, causing friction between BC Transit and the private tour operators, (who felt the public transit company was subsidized while they had to pay a Goods and Services tax).

Many companies train their drivers to give guided tours within the Gardens but during the 1980s this was discouraged, as passengers in groups of sixty or so began to block the pathways of the estate. Today, some bus drivers will meet their group at just two or three points around the Gardens, or leave them free to wander at leisure for an hour or two.

THE CHERRY AVENUE

Bob and Jennie, during their frequent visits to the Orient, had been enchanted by the beauty of blossoming cherry trees. They decided to brighten up the road leading to Benvenuto by creating an avenue, and on June 13, 1935, Bob contacted a Japanese journalist and businessman, Mr. H. B. Suzuki, and ordered 566 cherry trees in two varieties, Yoshino and, most likely, Mikuramagaishi. He then negotiated with the local municipality, as the road wasn't part of the Butchart property, to facilitate their planting. Negotiations would involve the Victoria Chamber of Commerce, Saanich council and the Liberal MLA for the riding.

Eventually, some five months later, the Minister of Works for the provincial government announced that the plan would go ahead. Municipal and provincial engineers embarked upon a scheme to prepare strips of land along the roadway for planting, at a cost to the public of around two thousand dollars.

Bob and Jennie supplied the trees, and by the end of that winter they were in the ground, and already being compared to the Street of Christmas Trees in Pasadena and the world-famous cherry avenue along the Potomac River in Washington, D. C.

Unfortunately, 1935 had a long hot summer, and the stream of Gardens' visitors along the avenue saw the young trees struggling to stay alive. The drought was having a severe effect on local farmland, too, and the question arose as to whose job it was to water the parched saplings.

By August, after six weeks of no rain, the situation was desperate. Following much debate, the Honorable, and by this time frustrated, Frank M. MacPherson, Minister of Works, strongly reminded Saanich Municipality of the initial agreement. The Butcharts had donated the trees, the province had planted them, and Saanich was in charge of maintenance.

Many of the original trees remain, having grown well during their sixty or so years, but some have perished, smothered by the encroaching forest and bush on the south side of the road. Some were victims of wreckless driving, and some were damaged or removed during road maintenance, snow plowing, or the installation of driveways to building lots which have since been developed.

Afternoon tea at Butchart Gardens - Jennie served 18,000 cups in 1915.

New cherry trees were often planted to replace those lost, but today, as you drive the one and a quarter miles or so to Benvenuto Avenue from West Saanich Road, you pass approximately a hundred and forty trees, sixty on the left side of the road and about eighty trees on the right. They range in diameter from three inches to almost a foot, and tend to bloom a little later than other flowering cherry trees in Victoria, coming into their own during April.

SPODE POTTERY AT BENVENUTO

Josiah Spode was born in the famous pottery district of Staffordshire, England in 1733, and together with Josiah Wedgwood, studied the craft under the legendary Thomas Whieldon. The name Spode soon became associated with fine tableware and in the summer of 1937 the company honored the Butcharts by naming a pattern of tableware after them.

The pattern, known to Spode as Hollyhock, was not

The Blue Poppy Restaurant today - a cedar tree grows through the roof and seventy water jets flood the rear window.

originally designed for Bob and Jennie. However, a custom colouring of the tableware, in brilliant blues and reds, was exclusive to the Gardens for many years, being handled by Spode's U.S. agents, Copeland & Thompson of New York City's Fifth Avenue.

Although attempts were made by Spode during the 1950s to rekindle interest in the tableware over a wider area, very little more was sold and the pattern was discontinued in about 1963. Technically, the shape of the pottery was known as Charlotte, and pieces of this dinner, tea, and coffeeware are now avidly-sought collector's items.

Apart from the official pattern record in their archives, the only illustration Spode has of the Butchart pattern is one

Coins in the wishing well go to
charity — was this a Rebel's idea?

taken from the Butchart Gardens tour guide of 1986.

Today, hand-painted Chrysanthemum and Rose plaques by Bossons are made exclusively for Butchart Gardens, and displayed in the gift shop and in the display windows of the tunnel which leads from the Italian Garden to the court-yard.

THE WISHING WELL

The wishing well at the south end of the Rose Garden is made of wrought iron and was brought from Italy by Bob and Jennie. Like most of the water features on the estate, it attracts a lot of coins. Visitors throw coins of all denominations and currencies into the well - to make a wish or sometimes just to make a splash - and the sight of such available change occasionally becomes too much for an enterprising youngster to bear.

Once, Jennie caught a local boy red-handed, stealing money from the well. She supposedly took him down to the house where she confiscated his trousers and awaited an apology, and his parents. It's not sure whether his pants were removed in order to dry them, or to secure his embarrassed presence in the Gardens, but as the story did the rounds it had a powerful effect on other young visitors. Money from the well has always been donated to a local hospital.

LOST, FOUND AND STOLEN

When you invite thousands of people, from all walks of life, into your garden, you're obviously taking a risk. Apart from the physical wear and tear on lawns and pathways, or the carving of initials on trees, some people had a habit of "collecting" souvenirs of their visit to the Butchart estate.

Before the opening of the seed store and gift shop, these illicit souvenirs would include hundreds of magazines, cutlery and tableware items from the summer houses and tea room. Visitors also picked flowers, stole seeds and cuttings, and ate the figs, walnuts, apples and other fruit from the trees, (fruit which Jennie used to give to local hospitals).

Youngsters took coins from the wishing well and someone stole one of the Butcharts' Pekinese dogs. Another thief, equally audacious, took a live peacock. Exotic and expensive as both these creatures were at the time, the kidnappers' motives were puzzling, as both are renowned for making a terrible noise. At one point, the Butcharts had around thirty Pekinese which would stampede from the residence and dance excitedly around any car drawing up in the courtyard, which was where the gift store is today. The car occupants would be instantly besieged until the noisy pack, for no apparent reason, would just as quickly turn and disappear back into the house.

For the most part, the Butcharts graciously turned the other cheek to this abuse of their hospitality, but when a statue of Eros was stolen from the upper lawn one dark night, Jennie became, quite uncharacteristically, furious. She immediately advertised that the gardens would be closed to the public. This caused an outcry in Victoria and many taxi and bus drivers, who couldn't afford to lose the business, pleaded with her until she relented, which she soon did.

Of course, Jennie Butchart and her staff would also find items left behind in the summer houses—coats, hats, mink stoles, cameras and umbrellas were often forgotten by people who were naturally more absorbed by colourful flower beds, or budding romance, than by personal belongings.

ROYALTY IN THE FAMILY

FOLLOWING THE death of her husband, Harry, which left her alone after a marriage lasting barely fourteen years, Jenny Ross sought comfort and friendship from her parents, and both were well afforded. She went on holiday with them, and one year, while touring in France, she caught the eye of the driver of their tour bus. He was an attractive, flamboyant young man, talkative in several languages, and he swept her off her feet.

He turned out to be Andre Chirinsky-Chikhmatoff, a man of high-ranking Russian pedigree—an erstwhile prince, no less, whose father had been an aide to the Czar. After a whirlwind romance the two were married in Toronto, Jenny adopting the new name of Princess Chikhmatoff. After a while they came back to live on Vancouver Island, but the prince found it difficult to settle down in the quiet city of Victoria. He seemed to prefer downtown nightlife to rural wildlife and was apparently more interested in socializing with high society than establishing a career for himself. No doubt he agreed with author Raymond Chandler, the creator of detec-

Four Butchart generations: Ann-Lee Ross and son Christopher, his great grandmother Jennie Butchart, and his grandmother Princess Chikhmatoff.

tive Philip Marlowe, who said after a visit here that Victoria was "dullish, as an English town would be on a Sunday evening, everything shut up, churchy atmosphere and so on." Prince Chirinsky-Chikhmatoff eventually left, returning across the Atlantic to live in Paris, leaving his Princess Jenny behind.

It was a difficult time for the Butcharts but the princess found support in her indefatigable mother. The decision to stay at home or follow the prince back to Europe was a tortuous one to make, but after much soul-searching she decided to stay with her family in Victoria. The brief marriage was over, but the royal legacy remained.

AN HEIR IS NAMED

In the summer of 1939, just as the noisy overture to World War II was sounding, Bob and Jennie Butchart named the heir to the floral throne of Benvenuto. Their grandson, Ian Ross, born to their daughter Jenny and Harry Ross in 1918, was now studying law, across the country at McGill University in Montreal. On his twenty-first birthday he received a call from Vancouver Island, telling him that he was now the title-holder to the world-famous Benvenuto estate. Ian was celebrating his birthday at the time and thought the call was a hoax. A second telephone call, however, convinced him of the wonderful gift, and the broad garden path that lay before him.

Ian was to quit his law studies, saying, so the story goes, that law was not his cup of tea. He did receive his degree from McGill University, though, one Saturday morning in May, 1941. But not without incident, due to his bookkeeping abilities, or apparent lack of them in those days. He gave the following account of this while addressing a convocation assembly at the University of Victoria, in June, 1991:

"We paraded up in order. . . to receive our diplomas from Princess Alice, the wife of the Governor General. So, when it was my turn, I noticed that Princess Alice was handing out circular tubes. . . and got mine, "thank you very

much," and wandered back to my seat. . . I thought I'd take a quick peek and see what was in it. . . so I pulled open the thing, shook it, and out dropped a little piece of paper like a telephone message pad, and it said: "You owe McGill University twenty-five cents!"

The war postponed Ian's stewardship of the Gardens for seven or eight years, but he gave distinguished service in the navy and was mentioned in dispatches. At one point, he and three of his cousins were serving in the Canadian Armed Forces. His mother, Princess Chikhmatoff, and her sister Mary, rallied around his grandparents to help keep Benvenuto in operation during the difficult years that would follow.

As winter drew to a close in 1940, Bob spent much of his time indoors, watching visitors walk around the Gardens. After giving his name to the nation's most popular private garden, he quietly confided to a local writer that he knew almost nothing of flowers. "Well, I know daisies," he chuckled, "and dandelions, and yes, I can tell a rose, but that's about all. But I love them all, they're so beautiful."

He still enjoyed the company of visitors, too, occasionally walking down one of the paths to chat with anyone he chanced to meet. "It's wonderful to have them here," he said, "I can't understand how some people shut themselves away from their fellow men."

For the first time in many years, the Butcharts had spent the winter in Victoria, and it had been a pleasant surprise for Bob to learn how nice the quiet season could be. "I don't think I've ever enjoyed a winter as much as this one," he told a reporter, " I wonder now why we went away every winter. There's no finer place to spend the winter than right here in Victoria." He and Jennie had travelled so much over the years that friends jokingly gave their winter address as "c/o *S. S. Franconia*," one of their favourite cruise ships.

At the end of March he celebrated his eighty-third birthday at Benvenuto, with his immediate family. However, his health was failing and his doctor was unable to get out to Benvenuto as often, or as quickly, as was becoming necessary. It seemed inevitable that the Butcharts would move back into the city where care was close at hand.

THE END OF AN ERA

As Bob approached his eighty-fourth birthday he and Jennie were preparing themselves to move out of Benvenuto and down into Victoria, to a house at 906 St. Charles Street. Their grandson Ian Ross was still serving in the navy, and was unable to lend a hand in maintaining the estate or taking an active role in its management. That job fell mainly to the Butcharts' lawyer, Mr. Harry J. Davis of Messrs. Lawson and Davis.

As wonderful as it was in living, breathing colour, Benvenuto as an enterprise looked fragile on paper. The annual cost of running the estate during the last year of Bob and Jennie's stay there ran to over thirty thousand dollars, and even after accounting for the seed company's revenue of some ten thousand this left a substantial deficit. The value of the Butcharts' philanthropy was finally being realized and the tourism industry was shaken to its roots. Even though a small staff of only fourteen or so gardeners were currently employed there, the estate indirectly gave work to hundreds more in local tourist and hospitality trades.

An editorial in *The Province* newspaper dated February 1, 1941 summed it up: "*. . . the Butcharts have been most gen-*

The *Times* published a poem by Mary J. Rathom in honor of Robert Butchart's 84th birthday.

*"Ten thousand throats
their joy proclaim
Amid those vernal glades
Where blithesome birds
unknown to fame
Peal forth from
emerald shades
A veritable feast
of flowers
Wreathe fragrance
far and wide
And sweet indeed those
fairy bowers
Where peace and love
preside."*

erous. They footed the bill for the creation of the gardens and their upkeep—and quite a large bill it has been—and shared the pleasure the gardens gave them with all who chose to come. Now, circumstances have changed . . . what with provincial and Dominion taxes, no person in British Columbia can any longer enjoy an income that will allow expenditure on the scale that the upkeep of the Butchart Gardens requires. So, an era ends."

A suggestion was made to the local council that the Gardens, in order to remain open, could be maintained by a cooperative effort from adjoining municipalities. It was pointed out that a "successful lunch and tearoom could be established" in the residence to help offset running costs, but to no avail.

There was the question of a legal snag in the Municipal Act, "which prevented the city or municipalities from contributing towards the maintenance of such property unless it was a park."

Everyone, it seemed, was afraid that the Gardens would fall into decay, or disappear altogether. But outside the Butchart family, few seemed prepared to do anything about it. The motion for local councils and the province to take over Benvenuto on a ten-year lease was never carried. It was alarming to realize that the gentle climate which helped the family create a lush garden so quickly, would just as soon nurture weeds that would suffocate years of careful planting and pruning.

Deer had always been a problem, so keeping them and rampant blackberry bushes at bay was going to be difficult. And clearing up after fifty thousand or more visitors every summer was another sizable chore to worry about, especially when the war had taken away so many workers and gardening staff of any ability were hard to find.

Bob and Jennie deliberated long and hard over what to do, and on March 27, 1941, people all over the city were relieved to see the newspaper headline: *"GARDENS TO REMAIN OPEN."* After years of welcoming people in to enjoy their gardens for free, the Butcharts had finally found it necessary to make a charge for admission. In order to employ a basic staff to maintain the estate, a charge of twenty-five cents would be made to visitors forthwith. (In April, Gardens administrators would announce that people in military service, arriving at Benvenuto in uniform, would be admitted free. It was a concession that would last for the duration of the war).

Three days later, Bob quietly celebrated his eighty-fourth birthday with Jennie and his family at Benvenuto, while the press published birthday greetings, citing his lifelong generosity and inspiration.

In the late 1940s, Ian Ross came back to Victoria and surveyed the estate he was now in charge of.

Under the minimal attention it had received during war years, much of the garden had slipped back towards its natural state.

The coastal forest and lush undergrowth it had been carved from some forty years earlier had blurred the edges of this famous landscape, and it was threatening to take over completely.

A family member once remarked that Ian took over "about thirty-six acres of potatoes and weeds."

But the spirit of Benvenuto still burned brightly there, and the acreage of canvas before him was ready for a vivid new set of colours.

It was the dawning of a new era.

THE MAN OF BENVENUTO
PASSES AWAY

For the last three years of his life, Bob Butchart had suffered respiratory ailments, and at the age of eighty-seven years and six months he finally succumbed to pneumonia. He died peacefully in his sleep at noon, on Wednesday 27 October, 1943, in the house he shared with Jennie at 906 St. Charles St.

His passing was greatly mourned and he was sadly missed by many. Bob had been a leader of industry, Free Man of the City of Victoria, a freemason, member of the United Church, past-president of the Union Club, a Kinsman, a member at several golf clubs, and honorary member of many organizations. But thousands, if not millions more, remembered him for his philanthropy, and for the beauty he and Jennie had created at Benvenuto, the estate at Tod Inlet that was now famous around the world.

A day later, a small private service for the family, led by the Reverend Canon Chadwick was held at 1:30p.m. at Hayward's Funeral Chapel in Victoria, followed by cremation at Royal Oak. His ashes were scattered on the waters of Tod Inlet.

Six months previously, as the war raged in Europe, Jennie had written a note on behalf of Bob to the *Times* newspaper, thanking them for an article they had published on the occasion of his birthday.

"He feels," she wrote, "that he is in the front line moving into no man's land to eternity and beyond, and that friends remain the best of life."

Perhaps this song, spontaneously composed and sung to Bob by friends dropping him off at Benvenuto after a boating trip, captures a glimpse of that friendship. As his shipmates rowed their way out of a peaceful Butchart Cove one warm Friday afternoon in September, they joyfully sang back to the tall man waving them off from the wooden dock.

> *Oh! Butchart, you're a friend of mine*
> *Oh! Butchart, you're a friend of mine*
> *May joy and peace attend you*
> *And memory oft remind you*
> *Oh! Butchart, that we are friends of thine.*

Though never abandoned, the estate had fallen somewhat quiet. Bob's bird cages were empty and silent, and his pipe organ found a new home in which to sing—a church in Vancouver. The Sicilian pony cart that once hauled noisy boys and girls around the lawns was now stored in the dark basement beneath the house. The toys were put away.

But a new era at Benvenuto was beginning. Every effort

was being made to recover from the lean war years, when gas rationing had kept many visitors away, and a shortage of labour meant that some areas of the estate were sadly neglected, and getting less attention than they deserved. Head gardener Bob Ballantyne had stayed on through the war, and brothers Stan and Alf Shiner, whose father had come to Benvenuto in 1918, carried on. Many of the Chinese gardeners had left, however, returning to their homeland or moving down into Victoria to start their own small businesses.

Both of the Butcharts' daughters were active in the management of the Benvenuto estate. In 1950, Princess Chikhmatoff opened the first commercial tearoom and visitors enjoyed the refreshments on offer, such as crumpets and marmalade for twenty-five cents. During that same year, the tile and flower pot manufacturing at the bottom of the estate closed down, but the seed company was still doing quite well. Butchart Gardens were still a long way from being financially self-sufficient but Ian Ross, now throwing heart and soul into his stewardship, had plans and dreams for a bright future. And this young man of thirty-two years had the energy, and leadership skills, to make them come true.

JENNIE BIDS FAREWELL TO BENVENUTO

Towards the end of 1950, as the days grew darker and the Gardens withdrew into their wintry hibernation, the woman whose dream they had been gave her last interview, to Canadian writer Leslie Roberts, from the *Saturday Evening Post*. Later, on the day of publication, millions of readers opened that magazine to be told that Victoria's proudest show-

The Butcharts. "Once upon a time there was a pretty young girl who got married and lived happily ever after." - Robert Butchart.

piece was not a magnificent sculpture or painting, but "fifteen acres of landscaped loveliness—known simply as Mrs. Butchart's Garden." Jennie, unfortunately, never heard the praise, as she passed away that same day.

Like her husband Robert some seven years before, Jennie Butchart died peacefully at the home she shared with her daughter Princess Chikhmatoff, on Tuesday evening, December 12, 1950. She had reached the age of eighty-two years. In preparation, Jennie had left instructions for her funeral, asking that it be identical to Bob's and just as simple—only one small spray of flowers in the chapel. And again like Robert, her funeral was arranged and quietly carried out by just her immediate family, within twenty-four hours of her

The ashes of Robert and Jennie Butchart were
scattered on the waters of their beloved Tod Inlet.

death. Before the public even knew she was gone her ashes
were joining the memory of her husband, on the waters of Tod
Inlet.

Many visitors to Butchart Gardens ask "Is there a monument to Mr. and Mrs. Butchart?" The answer they're given
is that the whole estate is their monument. The family believes
it is a fitting one.

TWILIGHT AT Butchart Gardens has always been a magical time. During Bob and Jennie's era, visitors were encouraged to leave the estate by dusk and household staff were often sent to do the rounds, removing stragglers from the tea house, or amorous couples who'd claimed some shady corner of this paradise for a lasting embrace. They could hardly be blamed. The heady aroma of fresh blooms and the sheer joy of such beauty had its effect on young romantics, holding them spellbound. Watching the moon rise from the lookout rock in the Sunken Garden seemed the most natural thing in the world to do, and couples often had to be coaxed down.

LIGHTING THE GARDENS

Although Bob Butchart had lights installed at one or two locations around the Gardens, a major electrical project was undertaken by Ian Ross in 1953. Lighting the four acres of Sunken garden was a major undertaking, and the main challenge was to avoid glare. "We want visitors to see light, not walk into it," said Ian at the time. A consultant from the

For the Gardens' 50th anniversary, electric stars and moonlight were installed around the estate. "If the light's in your eyes, you're going the wrong way."

Canadian General Electric Company, which supplied all the materials, agreed: "Moonlight doesn't blind you, and neither does starlight."

Around twelve 300-watt floodlights gave the gentle "moonlight" effect, with "starlight" coming from some two hundred smaller, cone lights. Seventy-five foot reflector lamps were also added for general area lighting.

A local welding company, Hafer Brothers, handled the fabrication and construction of the lighting standards and Vic Dawson, of Dawson Electric, was in charge of all the wiring. One of Vic's first jobs in the area had been to put increased power into the Brentwood Bay plant, almost next door. For the last six years he'd done various electrical maintenance jobs around the Gardens. But this was a huge task, the largest of its type ever undertaken in the region.

Apart from the design challenge of lighting such dense flower beds and shrubberies, and illuminating walkways without drawing attention away from the garden, the feat of engineering was nothing short of marvellous. Over two and a half miles of assorted wiring, plus over four miles of underground power cable, had to be routed around the old quarry, and hidden from public view.

Given the rocky outcrops, this was in itself quite a challenge and special permission had to be sought from chief inspector of Electrical Energy for the province, Lance Robson. It was the first time on Vancouver Island that a direct burial method had been used for laying such cable. The layer of topsoil brought in some forty years previously was still relatively thin, so workers were constantly hitting the old quarry floor. Ian and his staff worked long hours, often until four in the morning during the last week of installation.

In late June, when the project was finally ready, a full page advertisement was placed in the *Daily Colonist*, headlined: *"Night Lighting Project Heralds New Era for World Famous Butchart Gardens"* encouraging visitors to come out and see the spectacle.

The lights were first turned on June 25 for two hundred and fifty special guests and sightseeing officials. One lighting arrangement, placed under water in a pond of the Sunken Garden, was especially popular, illuminating hundreds of tiny fish, and suspending them like some eerily silent wind-chime. In the Japanese garden, coloured paper lanterns added to the atmosphere.

The project was a triumph and people flocked to see the Gardens by night. A few days later, however, turning on the lights proved almost fatal for electrician Vic Dawson. At lighting-up time the following Thursday evening, Ian noticed that not all of the lights were on, so he quietly set off to see what the problem was.

Without realizing it, Vic had suffered an attack of acute appendicitis while turning on the lights, but in an effort to complete the job he'd been crawling through the garden on his hands and knees, until he finally collapsed. Ian discovered him in time and carried him back to the house, immediately summoning a doctor. (By two o'clock the following morning Lawson was tucked up in Rest Haven Hospital awaiting an emergency operation, from which he successfully recovered).

Tour companies were quick to react to the brilliance of the Gardens' latest attraction. Royal Blue Line added a seventh bus tour to their schedule, called "The Sunset Special" which delivered visitors to the Gardens at twilight, just in time to enjoy the new lighting system.

A brochure was printed, explaining how to best appreciate the lights, and how to follow the route around the estate at night. Ian had a few simple words of wisdom to those who couldn't read a map—if the lights are shining in your eyes, you're probably going the wrong way round.

A quiet moment for mother and son at the Frog Fountain in the 1950s.

HAPPY BIRTHDAY

In 1954, the city of Victoria, if not the whole nation, was in love with its new Queen, Elizabeth, and the Commonwealth Games were being held across the strait in Vancouver's brand new stadium. Canada had just opened its first subway line in Toronto, and the warm spring atmosphere was charged. Benvenuto, much of its landscaping newly renovated, was a cheerful place to be.

One Sunday in late May, Ian Ross celebrated the fiftieth anniversary of the Gardens with an open house. At seven o'clock in the evening, visitors were admitted free of charge and welcomed with refreshments.

135

Recent changes to the estate were beginning to pay off. The rock piles and flower bed retaining walls of the Sunken Garden, built forty years previously, were overhauled and more top soil was brought in. Roses which had been climbing the quarry walls were carefully trained and repositioned. Shrubs and trees were transplanted.

Ian Ross also made sure that the Gardens were available to be enjoyed by all. He continued his grandmother's tradition of hosting visits from the Canadian National Institute for the Blind, (Jennie had enjoyed making word pictures to describe her flowers to sightless visitors), and over the years he made almost every part of the estate accessible to those in wheelchairs. Even though the Sunken Garden has fifty steps down into it and the Japanese Garden has almost as many, both have alternate routes that are gently sloping and without steps.

MUSIC ON THE LAWN
In the summer of 1953, Ian and his wife Ann-Lee decided to introduce music to the Gardens, and so began another tradition. The Victoria Symphony orchestra was booked and a portable stage was rented from Memorial Arena.

On one of the hottest days ever recorded at the Gardens, musicians arrived by bus and began their first practice on a shadeless, baking lawn. In an effort to avoid sunstroke they took to wearing paper doilies on their heads, procured from the dining room. But then the wind came up, doilies took off, and people went scurrying to find clothes pegs to hold sheet music to the stands.

The gateway to Jennie's private garden, designed by Samuel Maclure.

Black tulips, fresh from their morning shower.

The Little Girl - a polystone statue by Edward Apt.

Spring colour outside the Blue Poppy Restaurant.

A favourite food for deer, but 100,000 bulbs guarantee a show..

A temporary greenhouse protects the Fountain of the Three Sturgeons during winter.

Cement built the Butchart fortune, and now supports the rose arches.

One of almost 7,000 roses - a major attraction since 1930.

Chrysanthemum
ose plaques are
exclusively for
tchart Gardens.

Pottery wall plaques designed exclusively for Butchart Gardens.

Apart from decorating the Rose Garden, this wrought iron wishing well from Italy collects money for charity.

After almost a century, the orchard provides more shade than fruit.

The other Butchart Gardeners deliver a light touch of British music hall - a song, a joke, and a joyful parade of noisy kids.

A glimpse of Butchart Cove from the dining room verandah. The Japanese Garden sits in the hollow between here and the water.

Jennie Butchart's private garden and teahouse - virtually unchanged since the lady of Benvenuto last enjoyed it.

A hand-coloured postcard of Benvenuto barely does justice to the garden - but it would inspire George Eastman to invent colour photography.

144

The Victoria Symphony Orchestra marked the beginning of music at Benvenuto - and the end of the kitchen garden.

The first performance was a huge success, but, much to the Rosses' chagrin, the newspapers never sent anyone out to cover the event. Reporters simply phoned to ask about the traffic jam. It had been somewhat chaotic, and thousands of people had been turned away, not being able to find parking space anywhere near the Gardens.

However, the idea to have music in the Gardens had obviously been a good one and the following year vast improvements were made. A new side road was built to handle extra traffic and a one-way system was adopted, with vehicles entering though the new gateway, but exiting by the original hawthorn avenue, through the seed field. Ian himself lent a hand stewarding vehicles into parking lots, a job he'd enjoyed doing for years and was loath to give up. (He would continue his role as occasional parking attendant, anonymously, for the next forty-some years).

Improvements were made for the musicians, too. Gone was the portable stage and in its place, just west of the old orchard, a custom-made platform was built. It was surrounded by plywood faux pillars, to echo the music a thousand different ways and so approximate the conditions in a concert hall. This lawn used to be the old kitchen garden during Jennie Butchart's era, and the challenge of turning it into a concert area was met with ingenuity, and technology.

High fidelity broadcasting was still in its infancy, but sound experts Alan Macey and Dave Lindquist set up a small booth, hidden among the shrubs, containing a whole battery of Williamson amplifiers. Shielded by plastic, this electronic arsenal was one of the first public stereo systems heard in the area, and delivered a whopping (for the time) two hundred watts of public address system power into the air.

Special attention was given to the low frequency sounds, so important to deliver the full impact of a live orchestra, but local writer Audrey Johnson "was thrilled with the clarity with which string and woodwind bass notes came out."

Conductor Hans Gruber was well pleased, too, as were the crowds who filled the lawn, sipping tea and soft drinks and enjoying each of the four Thursday evening concerts throughout that July.

Around this time, a rumour began circulating that the gardens were up for sale, and that the interested party was the CPR. The story was never substantiated and reporters' questions at the time prompted the response "Poppycock" from the Gardens' lawyer Harry Davis, and nothing more than laughs from a CPR spokesman.

A few years later, various kinds of musical and light entertainment were introduced. Children were delighted with the pupper show and the pipes and drums of the Princess Mary's Scottish Regiment filled the estate with rousing music.

The song, *Fascination*, from the 1965 season's "Just For Fun Show."

A loud and colourful variety show, "Just for Fun" also took to the green stage and had visitors singing along to popular songs of the day, and chuckling at comedy skits. Two of the Butchart grandchildren performed here and one of them, Christopher Ross was hooked—he would later be responsible for an amazing series of fireworks displays that would pack the field with awestruck families.

Ian Ross and his staff continued to gain fame for their revitalization of Benvenuto through the '50s. Once again it was a popular tourist destination, though still very much a labour of love and not breaking even, financially.

The Rosses didn't live at Benvenuto, partly because their boxer dog couldn't be trusted to welcome visitors in a friendly manner. Sharing his grandfather's love of automobiles, Ian would commute from his home in either of two

The Rock Island in the Sunken Garden of the 1950s.

Kaisers, cars of precocious design among the first to incorporate a hatchback trunk. Sharing his grandmother's love of the garden, he worked night and day to increase Benvenuto's glory.

Ian effectively raised the Garden's profile and attracted visitors from across the country. During a national radio interview in 1957, he modestly played down his own efforts to put Butchart Gardens on the world tourist map, by saying the Gardens' fame occurred by "word of mouth, spread by friendship around the world."

He was, of course, right for the most part. In fact, just three years earlier, despite published brochures and advertisements (written by Ian himself), a Vancouver newspaper joked that the Butchart Gardens had a publicity man whose job was

*"Let me live in the house
by the side of the road
Where the race of men
go by
The men who are good
and the men who are
bad
As good and as bad
as I
I would not sit in
the scorner's seat
Or hurl the cynic's ban
Let me live in the house
by the side of the road
And be a friend to man"*

During Jennie Butchart's time, this framed verse used to stand on a table in the residence, next to the visitors' book. Today, several huge visitors' books are kept on lecterns in the covered area of the Italian Garden, and they receive hundreds of thousands of entries, in many languages, each year. Comments are read by the Gardens administrative staff and suggestions are often followed up, sometimes resulting in a building or garden renovation.

simply "to stop people writing about them."

Whatever the strategy was to attract tourism, it paid off. Ian's work with the local publicity bureau led him to its presidency on February 28, 1957, and it wasn't long before his mettle was tested.

The following year, the Black Ball Ferry went on strike, threatening to cripple the local tourist industry. The nearby town of Sidney, under the guidance of Norman Wright, rallied to aid thousands of stranded travellers from the U.S., many of whom were left to park overnight in a field off Beacon Avenue.

A makeshift food service was quickly set up at the community hall, and CHEK, the local television station, loaned feature films to help pass the time. But Wright eventually collapsed from exhaustion and was taken home, leaving Ian to take over.

Ian was quick to blast the city of Victoria's apathy at

If all the visitors that came to Butchart Gardens in a single year arrived at the same time, they would completely fill the twenty-five acre estate.

In fact, they would have to stand shoulder to shoulder using less than one and a half square feet per person.

The Rose Garden, as viewed from the wishing well circa 1958.

dealing with the obvious crisis.   In a *Daily Colonist* newspaper report titled: "*Victorians Let Tourists Down*" Ian said
the city had shown "a singular lack of interest" in the comfort
of stranded tourists.

In a jammed downtown Victoria, no long term parking
was available and authorities made the stranded travellers
move their vehicles every three hours. The industry which Ian
and his tourist bureau colleagues had worked so hard to
improve was in danger of being set back years. His skill at
public relations proved quite valuable in saving Victoria's reputation in the eyes of the visiting crowds.

Ann-Lee Ross lamented that children were cooped up in
cars during such hot weather, and praised the people of Sidney
and North Saanich, saying that thanks to their efforts some
tourists would want to return. The strike ended and the

Garden's reputation for sincere hospitality had been preserved.

Later in 1958, the Gardens were formalized in the business world, finally being incorporated as The Butchart Gardens Limited. Four directors were appointed, including Ian and his wife Ann-Lee, and twenty-four thousand preferred one dollar shares were issued. Benvenuto still wasn't profitable on paper, but it was certainly growing in the right direction. By the end of the decade, the B.C. Ferry company was running two trips a day from Victoria to the mainland, and many of the passengers had Butchart Gardens at the top of the itinerary.

A 60TH BIRTHDAY PRESENT –
THE ROSS FOUNTAIN

To mark the sixtieth anniversary of the gardens in 1964, Ian decided to build a huge fountain in the far south corner of the old quarry, which had been left largely untouched since the days of the cement industry. This area, the deepest of any in the quarry, had been fenced off for safety's sake since Jennie Butchart's time.

Using ordinary plumbing fixtures from the hardware store, a complex system of rigid pipework and spray nozzles was installed on a wooden raft, tethered to the centre of the pond and fed by powerful pumps. (Today, when the fountain is turned off for maintenance or cleaning, the raft and its maze of pipework can be seen, but a fine skirt of spray effectively hides this when the water is turned on.)

Originally, the raft was covered with a heavy canvas but

A sparkling gift for the Gardens' diamond
anniversary - The Ross Fountain.

after a short time of operation it had become a collecting bowl
which filled with water, became too heavy, and sank the whole
rig.

For many years this feature was known as The Sixtieth
Anniversary Fountain, but its name eventually changed to
honor its creator. It's now known simply as The Ross
Fountain.

The changing patterns of spray are based on a four-
minute cycle which plays "variations on a theme." When seen
at night under coloured lights, which are set to a three minute

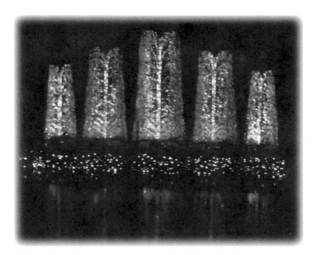

The Ross Fountain turns to "ice" at Christmas.

cycle, this makes a seemingly infinite display of changing colours and patterns. The main fountain at the centre of the raft shoots the water up to a height of seventy feet or so.

In winter, when ice could damage the apparatus, the water is turned off and the spray formations are cunningly replaced by clear plastic assemblies. These resemble icicles and ice formations around the fountain, reflecting and refracting the coloured lights and adding to the spectacle.

The walls of this part of the quarry are more or less left untouched by gardening hands, showing a selection of indigenous plants and providing a popular haunt for butterflies and small birds. The giant perennial Chilean Rhubarb at the water's edge dies back in winter, almost disappearing completely, but in summer its broad green leaves grow rapidly to a height of ten feet. Many visiting youngsters think it's the biggest rhubarb they've ever seen.

Tacca the Butchart boar — a friend to children and a burnished lucky nose.

THE BUTCHART BOAR.

This magnificent bronze boar, which the Ross family dedicated to all the children and animals that visit the Gardens, is a descendant of an ancient Greek marble sculpture, "Cinghiale," now in the Uffizi Gallery in Florence, Italy.

A casting was made from the Greek original in 1620, and it sits on the south side of the Straw Market in Florence.

In 1962, five more bronze castings were made by Marinelli of Florence, using a seventeenth century mould of the marble original, to which was added a small pool with plants, frogs, snakes and turtles.

Tacca was bought by Ian and Ann-Lee Ross during a visit to Italy over twenty years ago. "I was walking along the street just down from the hotel," said Mrs. Ross, "and there was a store that sold statuary. I walked by the window and was astonished—the statue was as big as the window. We discussed it at lunch, then my husband went back and purchased it."

155

By 1954, the Gardens were so popular a new road was built to accommodate traffic, as seen in this aerial shot of the period.

Another of the five bronze boars sits in Ontario, where it was donated to University of Waterloo's Descartes Foundation by a former math professor, in July 1978. There, as in Butchart Gardens, students rub the boar's nose for good luck before taking exams.

There's also a casting in California, and one more in Sydney, Australia, where people rub a different body part for good luck, one which Mrs. Ross didn't think was appropriate for the family atmosphere of Butchart Gardens.

Tacca also has two friends beside him in the courtyard: a pair of bronze foals. These sculptures, burnished by countless pats and rides, are very popular with youngsters. They serve as another memento of Jennie Butchart's time, when two Shetland ponies gave rides to visiting children.

DEATH OF A PRINCESS

Princess Chikhmatoff, née Jenny Butchart, daughter of Robert and Jennie Butchart, died in January, 1971, at the age of eighty-seven. Jenny came to Benvenuto with her parents when she was nineteen and spent several years working with her father in the cement business (and marrying one of his employees, Harry Ross). She also spent decades working with her mother on the Gardens. She inherited Jennie's artistic eye and gained a considerable working knowledge of horticulture.

The princess was also a popular society lady, often in attendance at gala functions, fund raising events and theatrical first nights. She was also one of the first patrons of the Victoria Art Gallery.

Her influence on the growth and popularity of Butchart Gardens has been considerable, but hardly apparent to the public eye. She worked quietly but enthusiastically behind the scenes, running the estate during the war years and opening the Gardens first tea room in 1950.

She supported her son, Ian Ross, when he returned from active service in the navy to assume stewardship. Until two years before her death, she was still quite involved in the Gardens' management but failing health forced her to take a less active role.

Princess Chikhmatoff
1885-1971

Princess Chikhmatoff shared her parents' love of travel, too, meeting her second husband, Russian émigré Prince Chirinsky-Chikhmatoff, during a visit to France. Her last trip abroad was in 1970, when she took a Caribbean cruise and accompanied her grandson, Christopher Ross, on a visit to Disneyland. Although she enjoyed the rides there she remained adamant in her wish to prevent Butchart Gardens from becoming a theme park.

FOUNTAIN OF THE THREE STURGEONS

In October of 1974, the Rosses ordered another cast bronze statue from Florence, Italy. It was the Fountain of the Three Sturgeons, which was installed during summer the following year near the site of a former summer house. Although it remains on view the whole year round, the fountain is protected during the winter months by a plastic greenhouse. The greenhouse also protects the plants around the fountain and on

The Fountain of the Three Sturgeons,
another Florentine bronze to mark
the Gardens' 70th birthday.

grey winter days, when little else seems to be in bloom, colour can often be found in here.

It is often referred to as The Dolphin Fountain, probably by those not familiar with sturgeon, a fish which is legendary in B.C.'s Fraser River, measured in the past at hundreds of pounds, and hundreds of years of age.

BENVENUTO IN THE NINETIES

EVER SINCE Jennie Butchart impressed her first house-guest with hospitality and her then modest garden, Benvenuto has seen an endless parade of visitors. Free tea had been served to thousands of people during the early years but the numbers soon became so high this generosity had to be curtailed. Before Jennie and Bob left the estate they were hosting around fifty thousand visitors a year.

Hard work invested by Ian Ross in the facilities and entertainment here, as well as his efforts to promote Victoria as a tourist destination, raised the figure again to two hundred and fifty thousand by the end of the 1960s.

A decade later the visiting season had been successfully broadened to include the early spring and late fall months, and around four hundred and fifty thousand were coming every year. The half a million per year mark was passed not long after that and in the early 1990s the number of annual visitors

The Gardens as seen from the air in the 1990s. Top right of the picture shows the reservoirs and fireworks viewing area.

increased to around three quarters of a million.

One year soon, before the Gardens are a century old, the one million mark will probably be surpassed.

*But who can paint
Like Nature?
Can imagination
boast
Amid its gay
creation,
hues like hers?*

The Seasons
J. THOMSON

162

Butcharts have a garden for all seasons. (But no skating, please).

THE BEST TIME TO GO

Until the mid-1970s, large areas of the estate were occasionally closed during the quieter months, allowing repairs and general maintenance to be carried out.

In 1977, an effort was made to welcome visitors on a year-round basis, with something for them to see whatever the season. Rarely is a garden or large area of the estate closed now, unless icy conditions make pathways hazardous or a large building project is underway.

Butchart Gardens is one of the few tourist attractions that is open every single day of the year, and it has visitors on each and every one of them.

With its mild climate and growing reputation as a conference centre, Victoria has a tourist season which covers almost nine months of the year, and it's been estimated that about one in every four visitors to Victoria makes the trip out to Benvenuto.

A concession is granted to regular visitors in the form of a one year pass allowing free entry when accompanied by a regular paying visitor. Unaccompanied pass holders pay just a dollar to enter the Gardens at other times, except during special events such as the firework evenings.

The Gardens' staff suggest that a late afternoon visit, after 2 p.m., from mid-June through to the end of September, is probably the most colourful and rewarding. All the food and concession services are in full swing, and entertainment is at its best. Although sunsets occur much later in June and July, it's still a good time to see the Gardens at night. A warm evening spent strolling the estate, heady with its scent of heliotrope, roses and night scented stock, seems to be a favourite pastime for younger tourists and the growing number of honeymooning couples who visit.

Early morning is also the time that much of the garden maintenance is tackled, though most of it is done by the time the admission gate opens at nine o'clock. Flowers have been "deadheaded," and pathways are swept and washed. The Sunken Garden, because of its aspect and depth, can remain cool and shady for most of the morning, and gets most of its sunlight after lunch.

JANUARY TO MARCH

This is a quiet period on the estate, when much of the landscaping framework can be seen. Stripped of their leaves, many deciduous trees and shrubs create space and allow views that are not available in later months. Frost can linger in the Sunken Garden, changing its texture by highlighting the lawns and providing a plain backdrop for a multitude of bright berries.

Apart from flowering heather, there's a splash of colour from crocuses, followed by early pansies, English daisies, and polyanthus. Primroses, too, live up to the French origin of their name, *prime rolles*, or "earliest little flowers." The bright red of holly berries continues to lend a festive air and brighten one or two corners.

Some of the earlier blossoming trees and shrubs include forsythia, jasmine, pieris and the early flowering Japanese cherries. By the end of March, hyacinths and daffodils are at their best and the earlier tulips, such as the white "Bestseller" are making an appearance.

APRIL TO JUNE

By now, all the signs of winter maintenance are gone and the stage is being set for spring. The tents and covers which protected some of the statues and fountains from frost have been taken away and the ponds have been cleaned and refilled.

Over one hundred thousand bulbs that were planted in the fall now fill huge areas with colour. The daffodils and narcissus provide gold and yellows, while tulips offer almost every colour imaginable. Cherry, plum and crabapple trees continue to flower, and the old orchard beside the concert lawn is in full blossom.

Around thirty species of other flowering shrubs add further colour, followed by brilliant azaleas and rhododendrons. The native dogwood, which prompts more visitor requests for cuttings than any other tree on the estate, is starting to bloom.

Early perennials are coming into their own by May and Siberian wallflowers provide both scent and colour. Forget-me-nots, a favourite of Jennie Butchart's, fill space beneath

tulips and the rare Handkerchief tree looks festive with its creamy white bracts.

Hanging baskets, bright with schizanthus, make their appearance and glorious cinerarias are being planted out. June sees the azaleas and later rhododendrons reach their peak while columbine, delphiniums, nemesia, poppies, stocks, sweet william, and tuberous begonias proclaim the arrival of summer.

In a few shady areas, near the restaurant and down in the Japanese Garden, the famous Himalayan blue poppy is now standing tall and proud.

Beauty bush, deutzia and weigela are also in full bloom, but by the end of June the Rose Garden has become the centre of attraction for visitors.

As midsummer approaches, the sunset moves around to the northwest, making the view down Butchart Cove (from the "peep-hole" through a cedar hedge in the Japanese Garden) a real treat for those who linger.

JULY TO SEPTEMBER

This is the peak season for visitors, but the Gardens gear up and hire seasonal staff to handle the extra volume. The heat of summer brings on most of the perennials and changing beds of annuals keep the riot of colour coming. Roses, both in the Rose Garden and the rambling or climbing specimens elsewhere on the estate, continue to offer colour and scent to the atmosphere.

Entertainment is at its peak, with music and dance being joined on Saturday evenings by the choreographed fireworks display. The Butchart Gardeners treat courtyard visitors to sing-alongs and light comedy, and encourage kids of all ages to get involved as they joyfully, but noisily, parade around.

By September, the show of dahlias and tuberous begonias is at its best, while asters, lychnis, and solidago fill perennial borders with radiant hues. Fuchsias and the large hydrangea blooms prolong the summer's glory.

OCTOBER TO DECEMBER

Autumn leaves, such as the flaming reds and russets of Japanese maples, raise the colour up from ground level, and the bright bark of native arbutus trees, or the rich tones of the huge copper beech near the Japanese Torii, pull attention away from lengthening shadows. The chrysanthcmum and dahlia show continues until the frost brings the first days of winter, and the first busy session of bulb planting.

CHRISTMAS AND NEW YEAR

Even though most of the blooms have long gone and many plants are in their winter dormancy, there's still a good deal of colour at the Gardens when Christmas rolls around. Visitors from overseas are fewer in number now, but many local families include a trip to Benvenuto as part of their holiday season tradition. A huge, well-lit tree welcomes visitors at the main entrance, next to the Butchart Gardens sign, and another Christmas tree, complete with coloured parcels, stands in the courtyard.

Lights tumble down the steps of the Sunken Garden's Island Rock like a blue waterfall. The Ross Fountain still has a changing pattern of lights which sparkle through the clear framework of "water" which seems to have frozen in mid-cascade.

Baskets of holly hang by huge red ribbons and amusing displays are tucked in among the trees - such as a "Joyeaux Noel" chicken coop, or the penetrating red eyes of an owl that sits watching a swarm of convincing fireflies.

Visitors also enjoy festive entertainment, as carollers in Dickensian costume sing and parade the courtyards. The Gardens' Christmas time lasts for the whole of December and the first week of January, and a keen frost (or a rare snowfall) can double the effect of the coloured lights.

The main entrance to Butchart Gardens flies flags of many nations, welcoming visitors from around the world.

WELCOMING HOURS

The admission gate to Butchart Gardens opens every morning at nine a.m. but its closing depends on the season and hours of daylight. The yearly closing time runs like this:

January to mid-March	4:00 p.m.
Mid-March to mid-April	5:00 p.m.
Mid-April to mid-May	6:00 p.m.
Mid-May to end of May	7:00 p.m.
Beginning of June to Mid-June	8:00 p.m.
Mid-June to early September	10:30 p.m.
Early September to mid-September	9:00 p.m.
Mid-September to end of September	8:00 p.m.
Beginning of October to mid-October	5:00 p.m.
Mid-October to end of November	4:00 p.m.
Beginning of December to mid-December	9:00 p.m.
Mid-December to January 6 (Christmas)	10:00 p.m.

In 1910, Jennie Butchart planted a row of Lombardy poplars to try and hide the cement works' buildings. Only a single chimney remains of the old factory, but the poplars are huge and healthy, lining the pathway back from the Ross Fountain.

THE TREES

It's not surprising that forests are a major natural resource of this province. Similar to its Rainforest neighbour on the west coast of the Island, (but a little drier) the area around Tod Inlet is classified as Rainshadow Forest. This is the most diverse forest type in the region in terms of total number of plant species. Layers of topsoil can be rich in nutrients here, but they can also be quite thin, and sloping ground which has been carelessly cleared can take a long time to recover.

Landscapers on southern Vancouver Island don't have to wait long for their plantings to take effect. In some cases, imported trees in the Butchart Gardens have grown more quickly and reached greater heights than they would have in their native countries. Many of the trees at Benvenuto have historical interest or a short story behind them. Here are just a few:

∾ THE ALBERTA SPRUCE
Picea glauca albertiana Conica
In 1904, when Jennie and Robert Butchart moved to this area and started the Benvenuto estate, this blue-green tree was discovered growing near Lake Laggan in Alberta. It is now a popular tree in local nurseries, especially during the Christmas period.

∾ THE BOLLEANA WHITE POPLAR
Populus alba Pyramidalis
This fast-growing tree was a natural choice for Jennie Butchart as she tried to hide an area of quarry wall during her early days in the Sunken Garden. Despite its relatively short lifespan, the two specimens Jennie planted by the waterfall about ninety years ago are still in good health. Landscapers must use this tree with caution—the extensive root system, relentless in its search for water, is notorious for blocking sewer systems and underground drains.

❧ THE CALIFORNIA REDWOOD

Sequoia sempervirens

Two of these grow in the Gardens and they were planted in 1934 by the head gardener of the time, Alf Shiner. His intent was to hide the chicken sheds near the Rose Garden, so they couldn't be seen from the house. Although these look like two mighty specimens that could hide an apartment block now, they are mere youngsters when compared to their ancestors. Redwoods can reach four hundred feet in height and live for over two thousand years.

❧ THE CAMPERDOWN ELM

Ulmus glabra camperdowni

When a Victoria grocer was clearing a lot to expand his supermarket in 1963, this tree was in his way. His wife, apparently, stood in front of the bulldozer until he promised to find a new home for it, which he did five days later, at the entrance to Benvenuto. Originally from Scotland, this tree is a weeping form of Scotch Elm and during its leafless season it presents a curious sight with its knotty, twisting limbs.

❧ THE CHINESE FIR

Cunningham lanceolata Glauca

This tree, its branches covered with dense, pale green leaves, is rare in North America. Its wood has a pleasing fragrance and in China it is used for making burial caskets. The brown bark is also used, to make roof shingles. Benvenuto's Chinese Fir was donated as a cutting from a local resident, after the Gardens' aborist, Edgar Dash, helped her with its identification.

❧ THE DAWN REDWOOD

Metasequoia glyptostroboides

This tree was once thought to be extinct, having died off millions of years ago to leave fossils in parts of British Columbia and elsewhere. In 1941, however, a Chinese botanist discovered a specimen of it growing in China. Seeds were taken from it and by the 1950s some of these reached Butchart Gardens where they were successfully planted and grown.

❧ THE DOUGLAS FIR

Peseudotsuga menziesii

Getting its name from David Douglas, a Scottish botanist who shipped its seed back to England in 1827, this stately fir can live for over twelve hundred years and grow to a height of around three hundred feet. It's a native of the area, growing in abundance around Vancouver Island, and is perhaps not as colourful or remarkable as some others on the estate. It does, however, form the far-reaching horizon here, creating a huge green backdrop for the show which is Butchart Gardens.

❧ THE GARRY OAK

Quercus garryana

This is the only oak species native to western Canada and it grows well around southern Vancouver Island, in rocky, sunny areas known as Garry oak meadows. There is only one Garry oak on the estate and this prompted Robert Butchart to have cement oak limbs and trunks made to decorate the Gardens. (These can still be seen today).

❦ THE LOMBARDY POPLAR
Populus nigra Italica
The original view from the Sunken Garden lookout was marred by the towering grey cement works in the background. Jennie Butchart formed an effective screen by planting several of these trees at the south end of the old quarry. Though the cement plant buildings were demolished long ago, the poplars continue to flourish.

❦ THE MAIDENHAIR TREE
Ginkgo biloba
This tree is one of the most hardy on the estate, and can withstand most pests and diseases, drought, air pollution and poor soil conditions. It covered most of the earth two hundred millions years ago, and hence earned its nickname of "living fossil." Its popular name comes from the leaves, which resemble maidenhair ferns. For centuries it has been revered for its medicinal and gastronomic qualities, being used as a treatment for asthma and Alzheimer's disease.

❦ THE SPINDLE TREE
Euonymus europaeus
A native of western Asia and Europe, this tree gets its name from the fact that its wood was used to make spindles. The fruit, which is spectacular in autumn, is deadly poisonous and has been known to kill careless sheep and goats which have fed on it. Crushed and ground into a powder, however, the fruit was once used to treat cases of head lice in children.

THE WEEPING HEMLOCK
Tsuga canadensis Pendula

In 1989 the staff of Butchart Gardens presented the Butchart's grandson, Ian Ross, with a pair of weeping hemlock to celebrate his fiftieth year of ownership. The purple-brown bark and gracefully arching branches of these trees are well suited to their location, in the Japanese Garden.

THE WESTERN RED CEDAR
Thuja plicata

This indigenous tree was widely used by the native people of Vancouver Island. It's durable wood gave them totem poles, shelter, and canoes, while the bark was turned into clothing, sails and rope. Visitors entering from the Gardens' bus parking lot can see a fine specimen growing through the roof of the Blue Poppy Restaurant. This is the provincial tree of British Columbia and is also known as giant arbor vitae or British Columbia cedar.

n the spring of 1991, Butchart Gardens was honored by the issue of a new Canadian postage stamp, showing a view of the Sunken Garden with the Himalayan Blue Poppy in the foreground.

A set of five forty cent stamps had been designed to celebrate notable gardens across the country, with Benvenuto being the only private garden among them; (the others were the Halifax Public Gardens, the International Peace Garden near Boissevain, Manitoba, the Montreal Botanical Garden, and the Royal Botanical Gardens in Hamilton).

Fifteen million stamps were issued and sold in booklets of ten for four dollars. A limited quantity of special souvenir edition booklets, priced at six dollars ninety-five cents, included two strips of the five stamps, a first day cover, and five postcards featuring views of each garden.

The booklet description, in both French and English, reads: "The Butchart Gardens on Vancouver Island was begun in 1904 in an abandoned quarry. It has since become Canada's largest privately-owned garden."

The images were the work of illustrator Gerard Gauci and designer David Wyman, both of Toronto and the project was sponsored by Environment Canada to raise awareness of Environment Canada week, June 2 to 8, 1991. Roger Wheelock, the general manager of Butchart Gardens, was presented with a mint edition of the stamp and an enlargement, both attractively framed to hang in Benvenuto.

The stamp was officially released on Wednesday, May 22, 1991 and the unveiling took place at the Royal Botanical Gardens in Hamilton, Ontario during its fiftieth anniversary. The stamps were only available to the public for six months.

An occasional visitor to the Gardens and a personal friend of the Butcharts was George Eastman, of Eastman Kodak fame.

He had a lot in common with Bob: both were hardworking, self-made millionaires who shared an interest in hunting and a passion for music. Like Bob, George took hands-on control of business, inventing the word Kodak, (because he liked the letter K) and writing his own ads for newspapers and magazines in his quest to "make the camera as convenient as the pencil."

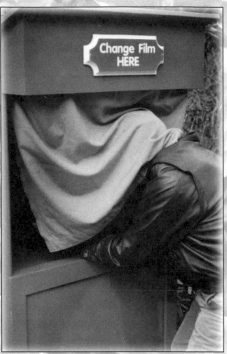

He, too, had an Aeolian pipe organ which was played every morning as he rose and ate breakfast, and he shared Bob's considerable philanthropy, by giving away thirty million dollars in 1930 alone, to several universities.

George was enthralled by the colours in the Butchart's garden and felt somewhat guilty that photography could only try to capture such beauty in black and white images. One afternoon, while taking lunch at Benvenuto, the telephone rang and he excused himself to take the call. Barely able to contain his excitement, he returned to tell the Butcharts that back in his Rochester lab, two technicians had made significant progress in a basic form of two-colour photography.

Unfortunately, he was plagued by a worsening disability (the cells in his spinal cord were hardening) and at the age of seventy-seven, George Eastman died by his own hand in 1932, just three years before Kodachrome film was released to the world.

It seems a fitting tribute that the garden George Eastman so admired is now one of the most photographed places in the country.

Visitors play "Name that flower."

FLOWER IDENTIFICATION

After years of fielding questions from visitors, the Gardens started to hand out free Flower Identification Guides. This sixteen-page booklet lists almost one hundred and twenty of the more popular flowers and plants found on the estate. Colour photos help visitors identify the specimens and a brief description is given alongside the plant's common and Latin names.

In addition to the booklet, a Plant Identification Centre is set up on a counter in the old garage of the residence. Here, small samples of flowers and plants are displayed in tiny vases, each with a label bearing the name. A staff member is on hand to answer questions and direct visitors to a location in the

Gardens where certain plants can be found.

Jennie Butchart certainly knew most of her plants by name and would educate visitors on her guided tours, but she and Bob were loath to label their stock as it took away the atmosphere of an informal, private garden.

Ian Ross has continued that philosophy and acknowledges that the Benvenuto estate is not a botanic but a show garden. The exception to this general rule is the Rose Garden.

FIREWORKS

The firework displays began in 1978 using the pyrotechnic expertise of the famous French company, Etablissements Ruggieri. The viewing area is a gently sloping grassy field, overlooking the nursery beds to the north and the lake and reservoirs, which were the old Fernie farmlands when the Butcharts bought this property.

The Ruggieri company was established in 1735 and though the name is Italian, the techniques were brought back from China via Bologna by a man named Ruggieri. Almost two hundred and fifty years later, in 1981, the world was seeing around six thousand of their shows every year, at an average cost of twenty-two hundred dollars per performance. Today's firework spectaculars cost about that much for just three minutes.

Jennie Butchart's great grandson, Christopher Ross, eventually became the artistic director of the annual fireworks show. He had worked for a while on the stage of Butchart Gardens, taking part in the music and comedy shows such as "Just for Fun."

On summer evenings, this peaceful lake explodes into colour as fireworks take to the sky.

An accomplished musician, Christopher spends a long time (and late nights in the old organ pavilion at the edge of the concert lawn) selecting the music for the firework display. He carefully choreographs the pyrotechnics to come up with a stunning new combination of sound and light, which will appeal to visitors new and returning, of all ages and cultures.

There is often a nature or floral theme to the show. In 1980, a sequence called Sweet Peas Bouquet used two hundred and nine separate projectiles, each fired electrically, shooting up to a height of four hundred feet. Such is the altitude of this explosive colour it can be seen by traffic skirting the Malahat Mountain, five or six miles to the west.

The popularity of the firework shows means that traffic is exceptionally heavy on those evenings. But technology, and staffing, help to keep things moving. Cars stream in from the West Saanich Road and Wallace Drive, and soon all roads leading to Benvenuto are filled with a slow-moving procession. People are encouraged to take advantage of the bus tours, with good reason.

A team of staff, linked by radio and equipped with hand-held stop signs control the flow at intersections and traffic leaving the Benvenuto is periodically stopped, while a Gardens' vehicle escorts tour buses past the line of waiting cars, down the lane that would normally carry oncoming traffic.

The whole procedure is monitored by closed circuit video and another team of parking attendants race up and down the parking lot on bicycles and mopeds, guiding motorists into vacant spots and feeding information back via radio to their supervisor. Not an inch of parking space is wasted as vehicles are directed to pull right up to planted beds and picnic benches.

The waterfront entrance to Butchart Gardens is also very busy on firework evenings. Dozens of people arrive in small boats, including canoes, kayaks and inflatables, to tie up at the dock and head up past the security checkpoint, through the Japanese Garden up to the concert lawn, to join the throng heading west.

The price of admission to Butchart Gardens includes the show, but the fireworks area is cordoned off to help direct the crowd. Bright green curtains, stretched between green steel poles, ensures that visitors enter by the main gate to the field, past an illuminated sign saying "Fireworks".

The raised lookout area is set aside for those in wheelchairs, and a few raised benches at the back of the field are reserved for VIPs and perhaps Gardens' staff assigned to videotape the show.

Visitors are encouraged to bring warm clothing and a blanket or groundsheet to sit on, though many are prepared to carry lawn chairs the few hundred yards from their vehicles.

Half an hour before show time the field is usually full, as thousands of people spread out, some enjoying picnic suppers. White plastic chains keep the aisles free but they're removed minutes before the show starts

The first firework goes off as soon as the sky is dark enough, though the silhouette of the willow tree on the island and the dark horizon of Douglas fir against a darkening blue sky make an attractive backdrop for the show's overture. The first performance, in early July, doesn't get underway until after ten p.m., but each week the starting time comes forward by fifteen minutes so by the end of August, the last show of the season begins at eight-thirty, (much to the relief of impatient youngsters).

After almost two decades there is still no typical firework display, but good use has been made recently of white Japanese lanterns, each lit from inside, spiralling down a steel track to float elegantly in the lake. Further tracking, submerged in the water, and suspended wires that disap-

For the Gardens' seventy-fifth anniversary, a special display was commissioned from leading pyrotechnician, Bernard Aubin of France. Sequences with names like Silver Flame Trees, Bumblebees, Silver Jumping Jets and Fountain of Pearls filled the sky that year.

pear against the dark night sky, add to the illusion, moving apparatus and fireworks in and out of view to great effect.

The mood can change from festive to eerie within seconds, by using flares to backlight the surrounding forest and undergrowth. The musical score has been introduced, on occasion, with a few words of narration, and classical music usually accompanies the grand finale, or aerial "bouquet."

The firework show lasts around twenty-five minutes, after which many people take the Night Tour of the Sunken Garden and Rose Garden, guided en route by staff members with luminous, hand-held sticks, (similar to those used by airport ground crew to direct taxiing planes).

Order of B.C.

Order of Canada

IN RECOGNITION . . .
During his successful stewardship of the Gardens, R. Ian Ross has garnered many awards, including:
1968 Victoria Chamber of Commerce Man of the Year
1990 The Order of British Columbia
1991 Hon. Doctorate of Law, University of Victoria
1992 The Order of Canada

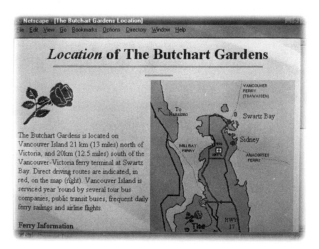

Since March, 1995, Butchart Gardens has been seen on computer screens around the world via the Internet.

THE GARDENS GO ONLINE

Like his grandfather before him, Ian Ross has always enjoyed using technology. The Ross fountain and the complex lighting system that brings the Gardens to life at night both demonstrate his innovation and ability to weave new ideas into the old fabric of the estate.

It seems quite natural, then, that the computer age began at Benvenuto some years ago and that technology has come to play a major role in daily routines. The effective operation of one of the country's busiest tourist destinations requires stringent control, and Gardens' staff rely on video cameras, two-way radios, a host of computers, modems and phone lines to keep things running smoothly.

In late March of 1995, the Gardens joined the Internet and posted their home page. Internet users around the globe could dial in by computer to see vivid colour pictures of the Rose Garden, the Ross Fountain, the Japanese Garden or the Sunken Garden. Of course, two-dimensional images on a computer screen don't really do justice to the floral displays and landscaping of the estate, but the information supplied with them is invaluable for those planning a visit.

Different pages on the Gardens' website tell travellers everything they need to know, from how to get here by car, plane, or train to what time the fireworks display begins. There's also information on hospitality and other services, how to book in a tour group, hours of operation, and what to expect when you visit at a particular time of the year. You can even browse a couple of items from the gift shop, print off a form, and immediately fax or mail in your order.

Feeding the words "Butchart Gardens" into any internet search engine will turn up hundreds of references, and many gardening clubs, nurseries, botanical gardens and tourism agencies provide links to the popular site.

THE SPIRIT LIVES ON

It would impossible to tell a story that spans a hundred years and covers five generations of an extraordinary family without some talk of ghosts. The spirit of Jennie Butchart, apparently, lives on. Many of the Gardens staff believe the residence at Benvenuto to be haunted. No one has lived in the building for many years, and it seems that no staff member is too keen to work there alone at night.

Many stories have been passed down over the years, concerning telephones that ring when they're not plugged in, chairs that are overturned, a billiard table weighing hundreds of pounds that shifts for no apparent reason, or lights which seemingly turn themselves on and off.

Several people have reported seeing a ghostly figure in and around the house, and one account that lingers concerns a commissionaire who was employed there.

It seems that late one evening, well after the admission gate was closed and staff had gone home for the night, he saw a figure walking across the courtyard. His calls went unanswered so, flashlight in hand, he followed the figure up the path and into the Rose Garden. As he approached the figure he saw that it was a woman, but he also saw right through it. The figure turned, and smiled at him, and that was the end of his career as commissionaire: he ran back to the house, turned in his two-way radio and quit the job there and then.

As for the ringing of telephones, it's interesting to note that almost half a century after her death, Mrs. R. P. Butchart still has her phone number listed in the Victoria phone book.

From trowel to tractor, Butchart Gardens' nursery in
the 1990s. Sowing seeds, and harvesting a legend.

COULD THEY BUILD BENVENUTO AGAIN?

Gardeners of all levels of expertise, from down the road
in Saanich or from around the world, have been to Butchart
Gardens and taken away an idea or two to use. No doubt
many gardens across the continent and around the globe are
the better for it.

Thousands of visitors have been introduced to gardening here, and bought their very first packet of seeds, garden
book or trowel. (It's easy to launch into horticulture and forget that maintaining this fabulous estate takes the full time
effort of more than two gardeners for every acre). But if
there's one crop that's freely available and always ready to har-
vest on this bountiful acreage, it's inspiration.

And the inspiration that Butchart Gardens has to offer
apparently knows no bounds. On May 12, 1995, members of
the Legislative Assembly of British Columbia rose in the house
to feed this inspiration to other would-be garden developers.

Here are excerpts from a speech by local MLA, Clive Tanner:

"I wish to speak this morning about an example of a community resource which is being recycled for the benefit of society. It is the famous Butchart Gardens. It has become the major tourist economic factor on Vancouver Island.

Quite frankly, we who live beside this wonderful resource are inclined to take it for granted [but] it illustrates to all of us how, with determination and imagination, a desolate natural resource can be recycled to once again be an everlasting asset. A lifetime ago the Butcharts realized that the raw resource limestone, having been extracted and used for our benefit, was not the end of the line. It was the beginning. In the first instance the quarry provided profit, jobs and material. In the second instance the quarry provided profit, jobs and a famous tourist attraction.

While Mrs. Butchart is remembered all over the world for the beauty she created, perhaps at home we should honor her today as the world's most dedicated recycler."

Fellow MLA, Rick Kasper, added:

"The previous speaker, I think, has touched on a subject that many of us appreciate, regardless of where we live in this province, and that is what those both in the private sector and the public sector can accomplish with a spent resource such as the old cement factory and works out at Brentwood.

Not only is it an incredible asset for the community of Brentwood and the member's riding, but it is an incredible asset for the greater Victoria area, and for that matter, the province. In many respects, the long-standing work and effort in Butchart Gardens can bode well for other sand or gravel-extraction mining operations of previous cement works.

What has gone on in Butchart Gardens and the beauty that is associated with it could bode well for the future of the Bamberton site."

EPILOGUE

THERE ARE lots more gravel pits and quarries, it's true. But there can be only one Benvenuto. A major obstacle must be overcome if the Butchart Gardens model is going to be attempted elsewhere: Robert and Jennie Butchart are no longer here to share their philanthropy, artistic vision and considerable fortune. Butchart Gardens was, indeed, a gift to visitors and was in operation for more than fifty years before it broke even.

Exotic trees, shrubs, and flowers are readily available at nurseries and garden centres across North America and today's ambitious landscaper doesn't have to drive half way around the world to collect a good specimen.

Certainly, technology has advanced to help the gardener in many ways, and watering systems, fertilizers and methods of controlling pests and diseases have all radically improved since Jennie Butchart's time.

But duplication of this glistening jewel set in a blissful Pacific island is, of course, impossible. It's not just the flowers, the house, the fountains or the statues. Jennie Butchart turned her homesickness and ugly surroundings into a tangible paradise.

There has been more than trees growing at Benvenuto for almost a century—there's been a legend. An enduring legend which embraces every hope and dream of anyone who's ever seen a bud become a blossom, marvelled at a dew-covered rose, or sat in a place where nature leans forward to gently kiss a tired cheek.

It is the blood, sweat and tears of several generations. It's the visionary leadership of the few, encouraged and implemented by the talent and perseverance of the many. It's the legend that is Butchart Gardens—and that's what visitors come from around the world to experience.

PHOTOGRAPHY CREDITS

B.C. Archives and Records Service - pages 22,24,32,34,35,38,39,
54,57,62,65,67,68,75,98,99,101,108,120,140,143,145,158,162

City of Victoria Archives - pages 29,34,41,71,84,109,129

William E. John - page 147

National Archives - pages 15,19,43,63,86,

Dave Preston - pages 1,3,4,9,31,45,50,51,52,69,78, 89,90,91,92,93,
94,95, 96,111,114,115, 116,130,131,132,133,134,135,136,137,138,
149,153,154,155,159,163,164,165,166,167,168,169,170,171,172,173,
179,181,185,186,

Darren Stone - inside back cover

Saanich Archives - page 104

Province of British Columbia - pages 156,161

BIBLIOGRAPHY (SELECTED)

A Better Life - the First Century of the Victoria Labour Council by Bruce Lowther.

A Bit of Old England - The Selling of Tourist Victoria by Kenneth Lines.

Along Mill Bay Road by Adelaide Ellis, 1990.

The Automobile Saga of B.C. by Geoffrey Taylor.

Beautiful British Columbia Magazine Summer, 1995.

Beautiful Gardens Round The World by Peter Coats, 1985

Beautiful Stoney Keppel Including The Village Of Shallow Lake 1855-1986 by the Keppel Township Historical Society, 1986.

Beyond the Island: An Illustrated History of Victoria by Peter A. Baskerville, 1986.

The Butchart Gardens Tree Guide, The Butchart Gardens, 1995

Canada Cavalcade by Robert H. Davis, 1937.

Cement in Canada by D. H. Stonehouse, 1973.

Cruise of the Calcite by John A. McCormick, 1973.

The Crystal Gardens - West Coast Pleasure Place by Pierre Berton.

The Empress of Victoria by Godfrey Holloway, 1980.

Excelsior! The Story of the Todd Family by Valerie Green, 1990.

The Forbidden City within Victoria by David Chuen-Yan Lai, 1991.

Fourth Entrance to Huronia (The History of Owen Sound) by Melba Morris Croft, 1980.

Garden Touring in the Pacific Northwest by Jan Kowalczewski Whitner, 1993.

Growth of a County Town by Melba Morris Croft, 1984.

The Geology of Southern Vancouver Island by C. J. Yorath & H. W. Nasmith, 1995.

A History of Victoria by Harry Gregson, 1970.

The Island Grower September, 1988.

Maclean's Magazine September, 1952.

More English than the English by Terry Reksten, 1986.

National Geographic Traveller May/June, 1990.

Oriental Occupation of B.C. by Robert McInnes.

Papers and Records by the Ontario Historical Society, 1920.

The People of Owen Sound by Melba Morris Croft.

Plants of Coastal British Columbia by Jim Pojar & Andy MacKinnon, 1994

The Portland Cement Industry in Ontario by D. F. Hewitt, 1968.

The Province (various)

The Readers Digest 1967.

Saanich - An Illustrated History by Geoffrey Castle.

Saanich Heritage Structures by Jennifer Barr.

Sidney Review (various)

The Science and Art of the Manufacture of Portland Cement by Henry Reid, 1877.

Standard Specifications for Portland Cement, Universal Portland Cement Co., 1911.

V. & S. The Victoria and Sidney Railway 1892-1919 by Darryl E. Muralt, 1992.

Vancouver Island Railroads by Robert D. Turner, 1973.

Vancouver Sun (various)

Victoria's Landmarks by Geoffrey Castle, and Barry F. King, 1985.

Victoria Times Colonist (various)

Victoria The Way It Was by Michael Kluckner, 1986.

The Canadian Who's Who. Vol 2, 3. (1936-39). By Sir Charles Roberts, G.D., and Arthur Leonard Tunnell, eds. 1936; 1939.

1001 British Columbia Place Names by G. P. V. & Helen B. Akrigg, 1969.

INDEX

Aerial photos 77,156,161
Automobiles (Robert) 37-39
Aviaries .53-54
Awards, Ian Ross 184
Bailey, Capt. Frederick 76
Ballantyne, Bob 128
Bamberton 56,64
B.C. Cement Co. 49
Benvenuto (the home) 101-105
Best Citizen (Jennie) 105
Best time to visit 163-170
Bibliography 195-196
Birds 45,51-54
Bleriot, Louis 13
Blue poppy 33,76
Boats .57-59
Brantford College 13
Bus tours 108-112
Butchart, A.J. 17
Butchart, Capt. G.M. 14-16
Butchart Lake 81
Butchart, Mary 32
Cement sculpture 98-99
Cement works 16-21,24-26
Cherry avenue 112-114
Chief Malahat 110
Chikhmatoff, Andre 119-121
Chikhmatoff, Princess 119-122
Chinese workers 26

Christmas time 169-170
Chubb, Fred 38-39
Citizen of the Year, 1931 105
Coleman, Dr. H.J.T. 104
Dawson, Vic 132,134
East Indian workers 26
Eastman, George 180
Empress Hotel 39
Fernie farm 21,63
Ferry strike 150-152
Fiftieth anniversary 135-136
Fireworks 182-186
Flower identification 181-183
Freedom of the City 83-85
Funeral, Jennie Butchart 129-130
Funeral, Robert Butchart 126-127
Ghosts 189-191
Gnomes .100
Graffiti .69-70
Hours of opening 171
Internet 187-189
Isaboru Kishida 29
Italian Garden 61-63
Japanese Garden 29-31
Just for Fun show 147
Kasper, Rick, MLA 190
Kennedy, James 11
Kennedy, Jeanette Foster 11-13
Kennedy, Martha 11-12

Laboratory 24
Lighting the Gardens 132-134
Lime Kiln Road 77-81
Lindsay, Hugh 33
Maclure, Samuel .59,61-62,86-88,102-105
McGill University 121
Mowat, George "Rebel" 109-110
Music 136, 145-147
Native Sons & Daughters 106
Natural History Society 52,74
Nicholls, Archie 70
Owen Sound 12-18
Paterson, Robert 12
Photographers & credits 194
Plant exploration 74-76
Plant identification 181-183
Plimley, Horace 38
Princess Chikhmatoff119-121,128,157-158
Private Garden 85-88
Railways .60
Rathom, Mary J. 124
Roberts, Leslie 128
Rose Garden 78,97-99
Ross, Ann-Lee 120,144,147,151-152,155,158
Ross, Christopher 147, 182-183
Ross Fountain 152-154
Ross, Harry 24,50
Ross, R. Ian 99-100,121-122,142-156,157-158,160
Royalty 119-121
Saanich 21-23
Salish .21-22

Scolli, Frank 98
Scotland 14
Seasons 163-170
Seed sales 70-73
Shiner, Alf 128
Shiner, Stan 128
Shipbuilding 59
Sidney 150-151
Sixtieth anniversary 152-153
Spode 114-116
Star Pond .62
Sturgeon fountain 158-159
Sturtevant, Butler 97
Sunken Garden 42-48
Symphony orchestra 144-146
Table of contents 7
Tacca the boar 155-157
Tanner, Clive, MLA 190
Tea room, first 48
Tod Inlet 33-36
Todd, Charles Fox 49
Todd, William Charles 49
Toronto 11-12
Trees 173-178
Troup, Capt. J.W. 59
Trout .44,46
Visiting times 171
Visitors' book 149
Wedding, Butcharts' 17
Westby, Bill 40-42
Westby, William J. 40-42,44
Wilson, Ernest 75-76
Wishing Well 116-117
Wrigglesworth, Joseph 18